All About Satellites and Space Ships

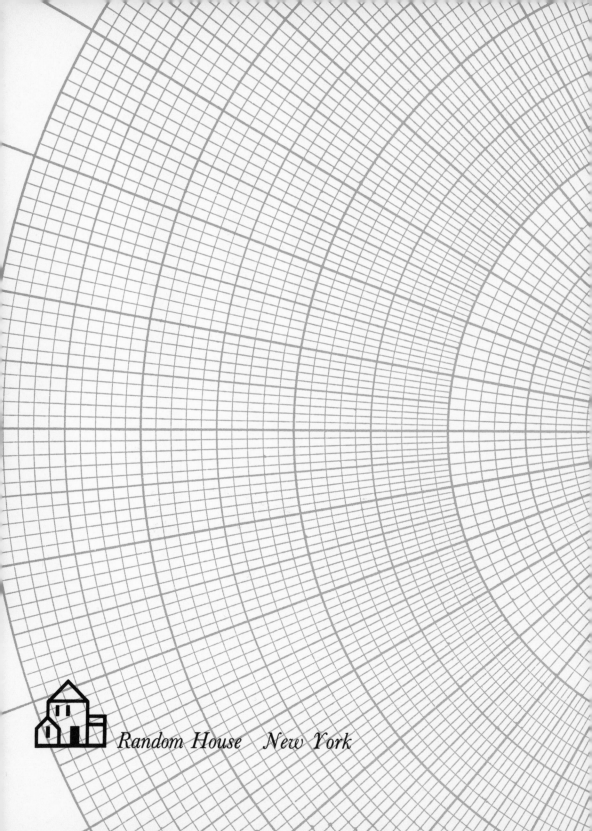

Random House   New York

All About Satellites and Space Ships

revised edition

David Dietz

illustrated with photographs, diagrams, and maps

For helpful suggestions about this book, grateful acknowledgment is made to H. Warren Plohr, research engineer, Lewis Research Center, National Aeronautics and Space Administration; to Fred L. Whipple, Director of the Astrophysical Observatory, Smithsonian Institution, Cambridge, Massachusetts; and to John Newbauer, American Rocket Society, New York.

Manufactured in the United States of America

Picture credits: American Rocket Society, page 31; Bell Telephone Laboratories, page 70; California Institute of Technology, page 45; Douglas Aircraft, page 28 (bottom); Jet Propulsion Laboratory, California Institute of Technology, page 101; Johns Hopkins University, page 67; Martin Company, pages 97, 105 (adapted); Mount Wilson and Palomar Observatories, pages 113, 117, 127, 134, 135; National Aeronautics and Space Administration, pages 10, 11, 20, 36, 63, 69, 79, 93, 129, 132; North American Aviation, page 94; RCA, pages 61, 64; Sovfoto, 51, 99 (left), 130; United States Air Force, pages 13 (adapted), 28 (top), 75 (bottom); United States Army, pages 17, 43, 53; United States Navy, pages 7, 39, 58, 59, 75 (top); UPI, pages 29, 99 (right); Wide World, pages 3, 41, 73, 81, 83, 85, 87.

dedicated to
Jimmy
Robby and
Jackie
three heirs of the space age

Contents

1. The Conquest of Space

Mankind stands today on the frontier of the most thrilling and exciting adventure in history—the conquest of outer space.

Men have already ventured into space and returned safely to earth. The first satellites carrying men into orbit give promise of the time when explorers will take off for the moon. Mars and Venus will be next.

The moon will be the first goal because it is our nearest neighbor in space. It is only about 240,000 miles away on the average. To reach any of the planets men will have to travel millions of miles. But once the moon has been reached, the explorers of space will be eager to take off for those distant, mysterious worlds.

Scientists are already forming plans for space ships that can travel the vast distances separating our earth from cloud-covered Venus and the red planet, Mars. Some of these plans are for ships propelled by present types of rocket fuels. Other scientists are designing novel types of space ships that will make use of atomic energy.

The Space Age began on October 4, 1957, when the Soviet Union put the first artificial satellite, or man-made moon, into orbit around the earth. It was a metal sphere about 23 inches in diameter, weighing 184 pounds.

It quickly became known everywhere in the world by its Russian name of "Sputnik." Never before had a new word become so popular and familiar in so short a time.

A radio transmitter in the sputnik broadcast a shrill signal. Scientists everywhere, as well as amateur radio fans, listened to its beep-beep.

Many other satellites and space probes have been sent into the solar system by both the United States and the Soviet Union.

The first man into space was a Russian, Major Yuri A. Gagarin. He made one circuit around the earth in a five-ton space ship on April 12, 1961.

The first American to venture into outer space was Commander Alan B. Shepard, Jr. On May 5, 1961, he made a 302-mile flight over the Atlantic Missile Range, rising to an altitude of 115 miles in a Mercury capsule weighing about 3,000 pounds.

A similar flight over the Atlantic Missile Range in a Mercury capsule was made on July 21, 1961, by Captain Virgil I. Grissom.

On August 6, 1961, another Russian astronaut, Major Gherman Titov, orbited the earth 17½ times in a five-ton space ship.

The third American into space was Lieutenant Colonel John H. Glenn, Jr., who orbited the earth three times on February 20, 1962.

There are still many problems to solve before the first party of explorers can reach the moon.

It does not matter how hard an unmanned lunar probe crashes against the surface of the moon. No great harm is done if an unmanned spacecraft becomes lost in space or if it burns up like a meteor on re-entering the earth's atmosphere.

But when a passenger-carrying space ship takes off for the moon, the situation is far more complicated. We must get our passengers safely off the earth. We must keep them alive on the lunar surface. Finally, we must get them safely off the moon and back to the earth.

The National Aeronautics and Space Administration (NASA), which has charge of the United States program of space exploration, is planning bigger spacecraft and bigger rockets to boost them into space. Before any attempt is made to transport men to the moon, unmanned lunar probes will be sent around the moon and brought back safely to the surface of the earth. Other unmanned probes will be landed gently and safely on the moon.

The NASA expects to send its first manned space ship around the moon within a few years. This ship will carry two or three astronauts. It will circle the moon without landing and then return to earth.

Later the NASA plans to land the first party of U.S. explorers on the moon.

Two of Cape Canaveral's many gantries. A tank truck (lower right) supplies liquid oxygen to the first stage of a rocket (left).

2. Cape Canaveral

A long ribbon of sand bars, coral reefs, and narrow islands extends along the Atlantic coast of Florida, separated from the mainland by shallow lakes, lagoons, rivers, and bays. About halfway down the coast the ribbon juts out into the ocean in a sharp point. That point is Cape Canaveral.

In 1950, it was a desolate triangle of sand dunes and swamps. Fan-leaved palm trees and a dense tangle of underbrush covered most of its 15,000 acres. Rabbits, deer, and a great variety of birds were plentiful. But so were the alligators in the swamps and the poisonous snakes in the thick underbrush. The only human inhabitant was the keeper of the lighthouse that warned ships away from the treacherous shoals.

The lighthouse keeper is still the only person living on the cape. But 18,000 people work there. Today, Cape Canaveral is the nation's chief launching site for trying out rockets and missiles and putting satellites and space probes into orbit.

To reach Cape Canaveral from the mainland, you must drive over one causeway that takes you across the Indian River to Merritt Island. Then another causeway takes you across the Banana River to Cocoa Beach. Once a sleepy village, Cocoa Beach is now the area where most of the scientists, engineers, and technicians of Cape Canaveral live.

A drive of six miles to the north from Cocoa Beach brings you to the entrance gate to Cape Canaveral.

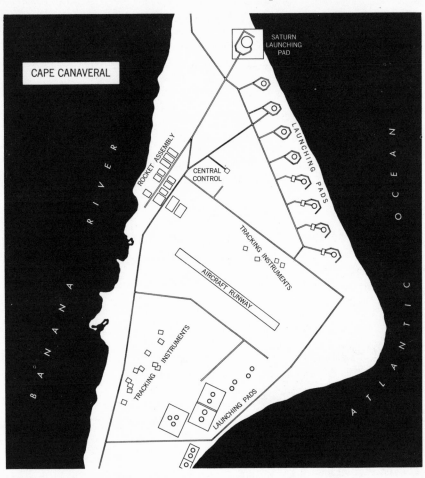

Once on the cape, you catch sight of a mighty row of tall towers along the ocean front. Built of heavy steel girders, they are painted in alternate stripes of red and white like gigantic sticks of peppermint candy. They are the great gantry cranes that lift the rockets on to their launching pads and provide working platforms for the crews that fuel them and prepare them for firing.

Near each launching pad there is a low building of concrete. This is the blockhouse from which the scientists and engineers direct the launching of a rocket.

Across the widest portion of the cape there is a broad airstrip on which planes can land. Beyond it is a group of large buildings which compose the guided-missile assembly area. High wire fences surround the buildings, which are heavily guarded.

Blockhouse under construction near a gantry.

Some of them are huge hangars where rockets can be assembled and stored. Others are machine shops and testing laboratories of various sorts. There is also a plant for producing liquid oxygen, as well as storage tanks for liquid oxygen and liquid fuels.

Not far away, there are a number of small buildings, some with domes on top, others surmounted by radio and radar antennas. These house the optical telescopes and the radio and radar equipment for tracking the flight of rockets and satellites.

These tracking instruments are not confined to the cape. More of them are scattered along the beaches both north and south of Cape Canaveral.

A network of paved roads through the palms and brush

links together the gantry towers and the various buildings on the cape. The undeveloped portions of the cape, unfortunately, still harbor as many poisonous snakes as ever. One of the hazards following a rocket explosion is that the flying pieces of red-hot metal drive the snakes out of the brush into occupied areas.

Monitoring Project Mercury at Central Control.

Near the edge of the Banana River, there is a two-story concrete building known as Central Control. It is the headquarters of the superintendent of range operations. He and his assistants direct the complex operations for tracking the flight of a rocket and recording the information received from it.

In a test flight a rocket carries more than a hundred instruments to measure temperatures within it, the behavior of valves and relays and electric circuits, the flow of fuel and liquid oxygen, and other important details. More instruments on the outside of the rocket measure atmospheric conditions. All this information is sent back automatically by radio. The radio signals may contain 16,000 readings a minute.

Cape Canaveral was chosen as a launching station for two reasons. One was that it gave access to a clear course down the South Atlantic between South America and Africa. The other was that a chain of islands extending down the Atlantic from the tip of Florida provided ideal locations for tracking stations.

The course over which rockets are tested is known officially as the Atlantic Missile Range. But the launching crews call it Cape Canaveral's "shooting gallery." An Atlas rocket fired from Cape Canaveral ends its spectacular flight half an hour later when it burns up like a meteor in the dense lower atmosphere 6000 miles from the cape—almost a quarter of the way around the earth.

There are twelve islands in the tracking chain. The stations are joined to one another and to Central Control on Cape Canaveral by a submarine cable. An order from the superintendent of range control can be flashed to all of them instantly.

The chain begins with the little island of Jupiter, just off

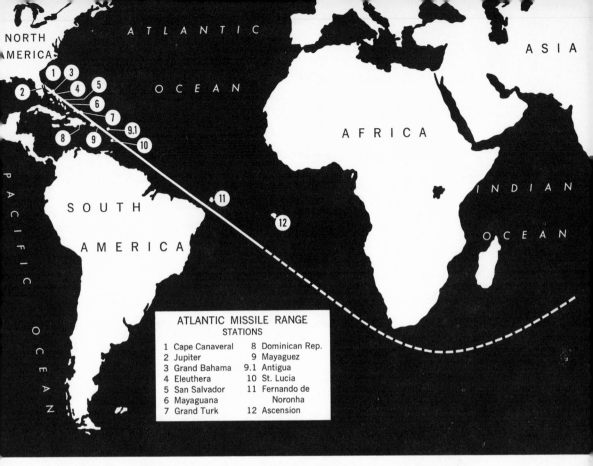

ATLANTIC MISSILE RANGE
STATIONS

1	Cape Canaveral	8	Dominican Rep.
2	Jupiter	9	Mayaguez
3	Grand Bahama	9.1	Antigua
4	Eleuthera	10	St. Lucia
5	San Salvador	11	Fernando de
6	Mayaguana		Noronha
7	Grand Turk	12	Ascension

The Atlantic Missile Range, where satellite-launching rockets are tested.

the coast of Florida. It ends with Ascension Island, a bleak volcanic island in mid-Atlantic dotted with extinct cinder cones and low hills of volcanic ash.

The flight of a rocket is tracked by radar installations on Grand Bahama, San Salvador, Grand Turk, and Antigua Islands. At Cape Canaveral, Antigua, and Ascension, huge saucer-shaped antennas, 60 feet in diameter, mounted on tall towers, tune in the radio signals from the rocket.

In the big gap between Antigua and Ascension, the observations of the tracking stations are supplemented by observations made by specially equipped ships. Airplanes are also used to track the rockets in this area.

It is a thrilling sight to see an Atlas rocket go streaking across the night sky over Grand Bahama like a thin pencil of flame. Sometimes, when atmospheric conditions are just right, the rocket will develop a long, shimmering pearly tail like the tail of a comet.

The rocket exhausts its fuel about the time that it is over the island of San Salvador. It is now about 200 miles above the surface of the Atlantic and traveling with a speed of 15,000 miles an hour. At this point, the Atlas kicks off its nose cone, which contains the data-recording instruments. Tiny braking rockets slow the Atlas slightly so that the cone pulls ahead of it.

Once its fuel is exhausted, the Atlas is invisible to the unaided eye. But it becomes visible again as it plunges toward the Atlantic beyond Ascension Island and burns up like a meteor.

The nose cone grows red-hot as it descends. It has a protective coating, which burns off in fiery streams as it comes down. As it reaches the surface of the ocean, recovery ships are guided to it by radio signals, flashing lights, and colored dye released on the water.

Rockets such as the Thor and Atlas, which are tested over the Atlantic Missile Range, are military missiles. But they also serve as the first stages of the multi-stage rockets that launch satellites and space probes. As bigger rockets are developed for launching bigger satellites and space probes, and eventually space ships, they will be tested first over the Atlantic range.

The range is under the supervision of the United States Air Force, with administrative headquarters at Patrick Air Force Base, eighteen miles south of Cape Canaveral. The range is operated for the Air Force by Pan American World Airways. The tracking instruments are operated by a subcontractor, the RCA Service Company, a division of Radio Corporation of America.

Cape Canaveral is not a military base. It is a station for testing rockets and missiles and for launching satellites and space probes. The NASA plans to enlarge Cape Canaveral as a base for manned flights to the moon.

Fueling crewmen in protective suits.

3. Launching a Satellite

Sometimes, when the word has gone out that a satellite is being launched, several thousand people will gather on the beaches south of Cape Canaveral. If the night is chilly, they huddle around fires of driftwood, waiting to see the giant rocket lift itself into the heavens on wings of flame.

Those exciting seconds when the mighty rocket sails into the sky are the climax of a chain of events that may have begun two years earlier when scientists started to design the satellite.

Two months before the launching of a typical satellite, the Thor or Atlas which is to serve as the first stage of the launching rocket, the other stages, and the satellite arrive at the cape. In one of the hangars, technicians begin the work of installing the guidance systems and the various instruments. They are also subjected to an elaborate series of tests.

The rocket stages and the satellite are expensive and complicated. They may cost as much as $5,000,000 and contain more than 300,000 parts.

The failure of one component, costing no more than $100, may cause the rocket to go off course or even to blow up on the launching pad. Such a failure may be due to a valve that sticks or an electric relay that jams. This, in turn, may be caused by a loose screw or a broken connection. Thus a faulty drop of solder can result in a $5,-000,000 loss.

That is why every component must be carefully inspected, every valve tried, every relay tested.

About a month is spent in installing the guidance systems and instruments, and in conducting the necessary tests. If any part is found to be faulty, it is repaired or replaced.

At the end of the month, the big rocket is hauled to the launching pad on a trailer pulled by a truck. The trailer is a kind of cradle on wheels.

Then the giant gantry is moved directly over the launching pad. The gantry, tall as a 10-story building, is built of steel girders. It consists of two rectangular towers of steel girders connected by a bridge of more girders at the top. There are decks or floors in each tower, and an elevator running up through one of them. The gantry is mounted on railway trucks that ride on two pairs of rails, one pair on each side of the launching pad.

The hook from the hoist at the top of the gantry is lowered on its cable and attached to the rocket. It lifts the rocket into the air and sets it upright on the launching pad. Great steel gates lock around the rocket so that it is enclosed on all sides by the gantry.

The launching pad is a platform of steel and concrete. There is an opening directly under the nozzle of the rocket, and below the platform there is a pit lined with plates of steel. When the rocket is launched, the flaming jet will strike these plates. A sprinkling system will pour thousands of gallons of water on them to cool them.

Launching of the Explorer VII satellite: After exhaustive tests (above), the first-stage Juno II rocket was placed on the launching pad (below). On October 13, 1959, came the blast-off (right).

The first week of this second month is spent in assembling the rocket's stages and putting the satellite in place.

The second stage of the rocket is lifted into the air by the hoist and lowered on top of the first stage. A score of technicians and mechanics, who have taken their places on the decks of the gantry, begin the task of fastening the two stages together.

The bolts used for this purpose are only temporary. Before the satellite is launched, they will be replaced by ones known as explosive bolts because each one contains an explosive charge. Shortly after launching, the controlling mechanism will explode the charges, shattering the bolts and separating the two stages.

But the bolts used at this time contain electric fuses instead of explosives. This makes it possible to check the electric circuits which later will set off the explosions.

A vast number of electrical connections must be made between the two stages. Doors that open into the two stages enable the crew to make these connections and to install the gyroscopes and other devices that will keep the rocket on course.

Next, the third stage is lifted by the hoist and lowered onto the top of the second stage. It is fastened in place with temporary bolts. All the necessary electrical connections between the second and third stages are made. Finally, the satellite and its protective nose cone are added to the assembly.

The second week of this second month is devoted to another series of tests. Now that the rocket stages and the satellite have been assembled, it is necessary to make sure that all the components operate properly in the right sequence.

These tests are directed from the blockhouse. Located some 750 feet from the launching pad, the blockhouse is built of concrete reinforced with steel. It has walls about 8 feet thick. A 10-foot layer of sand is piled on its heavy concrete roof. There are no windows in the blockhouse. The men inside watch the launching pad and the gantry on a closed-circuit television screen or through periscopes.

Rockets have been known to explode on the launching pad. The blockhouse is built to withstand an explosion equal to that of 50,000 pounds of TNT at a distance of 50 feet.

A tall, slender tower of structural steel, like the mast of a radio broadcasting station, rises near the launching pad. Electric cables run from the blockhouse to the top of this mast, and then to the nose of the rocket. These cables will be automatically disconnected at the moment of firing.

Now, however, they form an electrical connection between the mechanisms in the rocket and the switches and buttons and meters in the blockhouse. The members of the launching crew sit at a long row of desks known as consoles. A sloping panel at the back of each console is covered with the dials of meters. Below them are rows of red and green lights and an array of switches.

By closing the proper switch, an electric current can be directed into each of the circuits in the rocket. The quivering needles on the dials tell whether the circuit is operating properly. These tests go on day after day throughout the week. If any component fails to operate, it is immediately repaired or replaced.

In the third week, a static firing test is held. This is sometimes called a "full readiness firing." The rocket is bolted down to the launching pad so that it cannot rise into the air. The gantry is moved away from the rocket. The tanks of the first stage are filled with kerosene and liquid oxygen.

The crew in the blockhouse now go through the entire countdown just as though the rocket were being launched. This is the dress rehearsal.

On the count to fire, the test conductor pushes the firing button. There is a spurt of orange-colored light from the nozzle of the first stage as the fuel ignites. It is followed by a lashing tongue of flame that strikes the steel plates at the bottom of the firing pit. Clouds of steam rise as thousands of gallons of water are poured on the plates.

The test ends in 20 seconds when the fuel and liquid oxygen are shut off. But the crew, watching their dials in the blockhouse, know that the giant rocket has successfully passed the test.

However, the seemingly endless succession of tests is not yet over. Now all the components of the rocket assembly have to be tested again to make sure that they have withstood the vibration and strain of the firing test. If anything is found out of adjustment, it must be corrected at once.

As the fourth week of the month arrives, the blockhouse crew gets ready for the actual launching.

At last a day is set. The state of the weather is watched carefully, to make sure that no high winds will interfere.

The countdown begins eight hours before the moment agreed upon for launching. That moment is known as T for "test time." The time of each operation is figured backward from T. Therefore, the countdown begins at T-minus-8-hours. This is announced over the loudspeakers in the blockhouse and in the launching area as the countdown begins.

Members of the gantry crew man the decks to make any last-minute adjustments required as the countdown proceeds. In the blockhouse, the director of operations—known as the test conductor—has a list of a thousand items that must be checked one by one.

An assistant reads each item into the microphone. At one of the consoles, an engineer closes the proper switches and watches the swinging needles on his dials. If the test is satisfactory, he pushes a button that lights a green light on the conductor's desk.

If the test fails, the engineer pushes another button that switches on a red light. Then the countdown stops until the trouble has been located and the necessary correction made.

If this happens, the timekeeper announces the news over

the loudspeakers, calling out "Holding on T-minus-6-hours," if that happens to be the time. When the trouble has been eliminated, he resumes the countdown by announcing "T-minus-6-hours and counting."

As the sun goes down and the darkness gathers, giant floodlights are turned on in the launching area. The great gantry blossoms out with an array of several hundred electric lights, most of them white, but a few green or red.

At T-minus-3-hours, the gantry crew begins the hazardous task of replacing the fused bolts with explosive bolts. The launching area is cleared of all persons not directly engaged in this operation. As each explosive bolt is put in place, the necessary electrical connections are made to the charge.

Next, a large explosive charge is placed in the first stage of the rocket. This is known as the "destruct charge."

When the rocket is fired, radars will track it, automatically feeding the information to electronic computers which will plot its course from second to second. This information will appear on dials on one of the consoles in Central Control. The range safety officer will stand at this console, watching the dials. If the rocket goes off course, he will push a red button known as the "destruct button." A radio impulse will flash to the rocket, setting in motion a chain of events that will detonate the "destruct charge" and destroy the rocket.

At T-minus-1½-hours, the fueling operation begins. Every-

Finally, "Five . . . four . . . three . . . two . . . one . . . FIRE!"

The test conductor pushes the firing button, starting the sequence of operations within the rocket that will send it on its way into outer space. For a few seconds nothing seems to happen. Then the electric cable drops from the nose of the rocket and swings down against its supporting mast. There is a bright flash at the base of the rocket, followed by a mighty roar as the fuel begins to burn.

A shrill, piercing wail, like that of a siren, is added to the noise as the turbine and pumps of the first stage reach full speed.

The flaming gases, emerging from the nozzle of the first stage, are deflected sideways by the steel plates of the firing pit. Great clouds of steam form as the sprinkling system pours thousands of gallons of water upon these plates. The rocket is all but hidden by the billowing clouds which glow with a fitful, eerie light as they reflect the rocket's flaming jet.

Now the rocket begins to rise— but slowly. To the watchers on the

Launching of the Echo I satellite by a three-stage Thor-Delta rocket.

Path of the rocket that launched Pioneer I, shown in a time exposure.

beach, it seems to be standing still. "Go," they shout, "go, go, go!"

For a few seconds, the rocket seems to be balancing itself on the pillar of fire emerging from the nozzle of its motor. But now it picks up speed, and the pillar is turned into a lashing fiery tail. The tail is intensely bright and it flutters violently as the rocket gathers speed and sets itself on its course.

At an altitude of a thousand feet, it lights up the sea below and the underside of the clouds above. The rocket continues to rise and as it disappears into the distance, it grows fainter and fainter.

The crowds on the beach are excited and jubilant. There is no anxiety in their voices now as they shout, "Go! Go! Go!"

Robert H. Goddard with the first successful liquid-fuel rocket.

4. From Fireworks to Satellites

The giant space ship that may take you to the moon some day will be a descendant of the satellites and space probes now circling the earth and the sun. And the rockets that put the space ship into orbit will be descendants of the spectacular fireworks that go zooming into the sky at Fourth of July celebrations.

Anyone who understands how skyrockets work will have no difficulty in understanding rockets of any kind.

The simplest skyrocket consists of a little cardboard tube, five or six inches long, mounted on the top of a thin stick. The tube is filled with gunpowder and has a fuse at the bottom.

Rockets like this were made by the Chinese more than seven hundred years ago. The Chinese used them to frighten and drive away enemies as well as for fireworks.

Long ago the Chinese made improvements in the design of their rockets which are still found in fireworks rockets today. One of these was to put a cone on the top of the rocket so that it had a pointed end. This made the rocket fly better.

The Chinese also found that an extra charge of powder could be put in the pointed end and made to explode when the rocket landed among enemy troops. Today the cone of a fireworks rocket is loaded with colored stars.

The other improvement made by the Chinese was to scoop out a hole in the back of the powder charge. This made the powder burn faster, and so the rocket went faster. If a simple fireworks rocket were sliced open lengthwise, it would look like this:

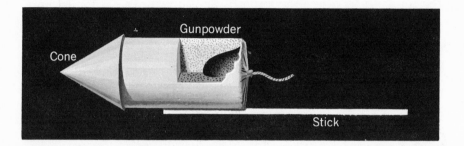

The secret of making rockets was learned by the Arabs from the Chinese, and by the nations of Europe from the Arabs. Soon all the armies of Europe were using rockets. But by the year 1500 rockets had been given up in favor of cannon.

Improved rockets came back into use about 1800. The British used rockets against the United States in the War of 1812. In "The Star-Spangled Banner" you sing of "the rockets' red glare."

The behavior of a rocket is explained by a scientific law formulated by the great Sir Isaac Newton. It is known as Newton's third law of motion. This law states: To every action there is an equal and opposite reaction.

If you have watched someone dive from a small float, you may have noticed that the raft dips into the water as the diver rises into the air. The downward movement of the raft is the reaction to the upward movement of the diver.

If you have fired a rifle, you will remember that the gun kicked against your shoulder. This kick is the recoil of the gun. It is the reaction of the gun to the forward motion of the bullet.

In the same fashion, the forward motion of the rocket is the reaction to the backward motion of the train of escaping gases, like this:

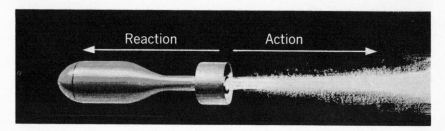

By about 1850 the armies of the world had given up rockets once more. At the start of the twentieth century, rockets did not seem very important.

This was changed by an American scientist who was shy and retiring, brilliant and hard-working. He gave his whole career to research on rockets. He was Dr. Robert Hutchins Goddard, professor of physics at Clark University in Worcester, Massachusetts. He is remembered as the father of modern rocketry.

Dr. Goddard's experiments proved that the speed of a rocket depends upon the speed with which the train of burning gases is ejected from it. He soon realized that he could not build the kind of rocket he wanted with gunpowder as a fuel. So he turned his attention to liquid fuels.

On March 16, 1926, Goddard launched the first successful rocket using liquid fuel. This took place in the little town of Auburn, Massachusetts, on a snow-covered field of a farm owned by one of his relatives.

The rocket was a very light affair about 10 feet long. It used gasoline and liquid oxygen. A liquid-fuel rocket cannot draw its oxygen from the air as an automobile engine or airplane engine does. It must carry its own oxygen.

The little rocket stayed in the air for two and a half seconds and traveled a distance of 184 feet. That doesn't sound like much, but it was a beginning.

Goddard continued to work on liquid-fuel rockets. His researches were supported by the Guggenheim Foundation and the Smithsonian Institution. Meanwhile other scientists and amateur enthusiasts entered the field, and rocket societies were formed in many countries, including the United States, England, and Germany.

Before World War II, the German Army started a rocket program. Finally a huge establishment was built at Peenemünde on the Baltic Sea. Here the V-2 rocket was developed.

The first V-2 rocket fell on London on September 8, 1944. In the next seven months more than a thousand of them landed in or near London, killing about two thousand people and doing much damage. No defense against the V-2 was developed during World War II.

The V-2 was a rocket 46 feet long, weighing 14 tons. Its

Scout rocket: After the first two stages are bolted together and raised on the pad (left), the third stage is lifted into position (right). A fourth stage is added, and then the Scout is launched (below).

warhead weighed one ton. Most of the rocket's weight was in its propellants. It carried four tons of ethyl alcohol and five tons of liquid oxygen.

At the close of World War II, American troops captured a large number of V-2 rockets. These were used to start high-altitude researches at the White Sands Proving Ground in New Mexico.

In 1949, a two-stage rocket, consisting of a V-2 with a slim rocket 16 feet long, known as the WAC Corporal, mounted on its nose, was fired at White Sands. The WAC Corporal reached an altitude of 244 miles. This was a history-making event because no rocket had previously reached such an altitude.

Following the experience with the V-2 rockets, the Armed Forces embarked upon the development of a number of big rockets as military weapons. However, a number of them have been used as the first stages of multi-stage rockets for the launching of satellites and space probes. These include the Redstone, Jupiter, Thor, and Atlas.

The National Aeronautics and Space Administration has developed a four-stage rocket known as the Scout. All its stages employ solid fuel. For launching moderate-sized satellites, the Scout is more economical than the rockets employing liquid-fuel first stages.

It is interesting to compare Goddard's first little liquid-fuel rocket with the giant rockets of today. Progress has been truly amazing. But, as we shall see, even bigger rockets are planned for the future.

5. First Satellites Into Space

Soon after World War II, American and European scientists began thinking about the possibility of putting up man-made satellites. The subject was discussed in London in 1950 at the Second Congress of the International Astronautical Federation. Soon after, the American Rocket Society formed a committee to consider the possibility.

Designs for a satellite were presented by Dr. S. Fred Singer, rocket expert of the University of Maryland, at a conference in Oxford, England, in August 1953. He proposed a satellite about the size of a basketball. It would contain scientific instruments like the ones that had previously been carried up in the noses of high-altitude rockets. Automatic radio transmitters would send the readings of these instruments back to earth.

In the summer of 1954 a group of rocket experts met with high-ranking Army and Navy officers in Washington. A plan for launching a five-pound satellite was proposed by Dr. Wernher von Braun. He called it Project Orbiter.

Dr. von Braun and his colleagues had developed a military rocket for the Army. Known as the Redstone and patterned after the V-2, it carried a five-ton warhead. Dr. von Braun's plan was to replace the warhead with a cluster of solid-fuel rockets.

A few months later, a special committee of the International Geophysical Year asked the governments concerned to consider launching satellites during the IGY.

The Army wanted to go ahead with Project Orbiter. The

Navy wished to build a three-stage rocket using the Viking rocket as the first stage. On July 29, 1955, the White House announced that the satellite project had been assigned to the Navy and that it would be known as Project Vanguard. A schedule was set up, calling for the launching of the first U.S. satellite in November 1957.

Meanwhile, it became known that the Soviet Union was also making plans to launch a satellite. The Russians had used small rockets as artillery weapons in World War II. They had continued their development of rockets after the war.

The Soviet Union achieved the historic honor of inaugurating the Age of Space by putting the first satellite into orbit. Sputnik I was launched on October 4, 1957. Its first beep was picked up by radio in the United States at 8:07 that evening.

Models of Sputnik I (near the roof) and Sputnik II (foreground).

Sputnik I had been launched by a three-stage rocket. Made of highly polished aluminum, the satellite was 23 inches in diameter and weighed 184 pounds. Four metal rods protruding from it served as radio antennas. The sputnik contained instruments for measuring temperatures, pressures, cosmic rays, and the impact of meteors.

Sputnik II was launched on November 3, 1957. This was an even more startling revelation of the great progress which Russia had made in the development of rockets. It weighed 1,120 pounds—more than half a ton. It was shaped like a cone and carried instruments to make various measurements including the ultraviolet radiations of the sun and the cosmic rays. It remained attached to the third stage of the launching rocket.

The biggest surprise of all was that it contained a dog as a passenger. The dog was a small-boned Eskimo dog of a type known as a laika.

The dog was in a sealed compartment which contained air-conditioning equipment and a stock of food. Instruments recorded the dog's breathing, pulse rate, and blood pressure. This equipment was connected to the sputnik's radio so that information about the condition of the dog was broadcast to receiving stations on the ground. The dog remained alive for a week.

There was a great deal of discussion of the American rocket program in Congress and in the newspapers. One result was that the Department of Defense told the Army to go ahead with Project Orbiter.

Army experts set up their rocket at Cape Canaveral. It was a four-stage Jupiter-C rocket, designed by Dr. von Braun and his colleagues. It stood 68½ feet high. On January 31, 1958, this rocket launched the first made-in-America satellite, known as Explorer I. It was 40 inches long and six inches in diameter. This was the same size as the empty shell of the fourth stage, which was permanently attached to it. The two together weighed 31 pounds.

The Navy's first Vanguard satellite, known as Vanguard I, was launched on March 17, 1958. It was a metal sphere, only 6 inches in diameter. The launching was unusually successful, the satellite attaining an exceptionally high orbit.

At its lowest point it is 410 miles above the earth. At its highest point it is 2,450 miles up. Because it encounters so little atmospheric drag, scientists expect Vanguard I to remain in orbit for decades, perhaps for as long as 100 or 200 years.

Explorer I, first U.S. satellite, was launched on January 31, 1958.

These first satellites in orbit around the earth amply justified their cost. Each new satellite put into space has given scientists additional information about the earth and the solar system.

Pioneer IV, man-made planet whose orbit lies between those of earth and of Mars. The fiberglas cone, washed with gold, served as the space probe's antenna.

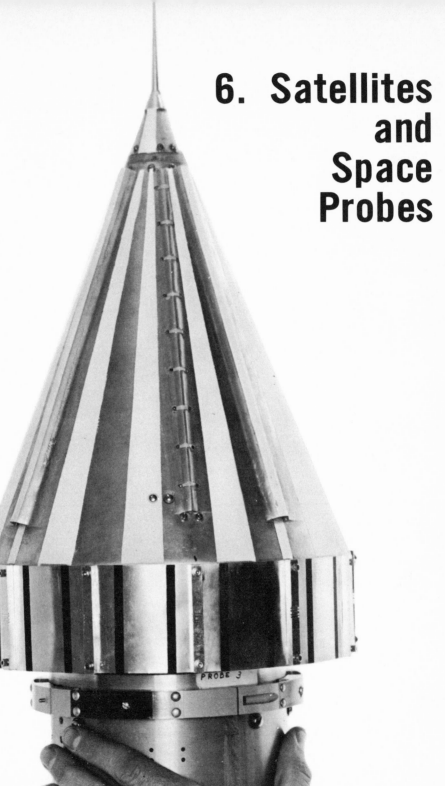

6. Satellites and Space Probes

As soon as Sputnik I was in the sky, people began to ask questions. One question often asked was: What keeps the sputnik going?

The answer is that a satellite keeps going because there is nothing to stop it.

To understand this, we must have a look at Newton's three laws of motion. You will remember that Newton's third law of motion explains what makes a rocket go. This law states that every action has an equal and opposite reaction.

Now we need the first two laws of motion. Newton's first law states: Every body continues in its state of rest or uniform motion in a straight line unless acted on by some force.

In other words, a body, once set in motion, will keep going forever, unless it encounters some force that opposes its motion.

Newton's second law tells us that any change in speed or direction of a moving body depends upon the magnitude of the force acting on it and the length of time it acts.

This explains why the pull of the earth's gravity keeps both the moon and the artificial satellites in their orbits. If there were no force of gravity, they would all fly off into space.

If a satellite had no motion of its own, the earth's force of gravity would pull it straight down.

It is the combination of the two that keeps the satellite

in its orbit. At the same time that the satellite is moving forward, it is falling toward the earth.

The combination keeps the satellite going around the earth, as shown in the following diagram:

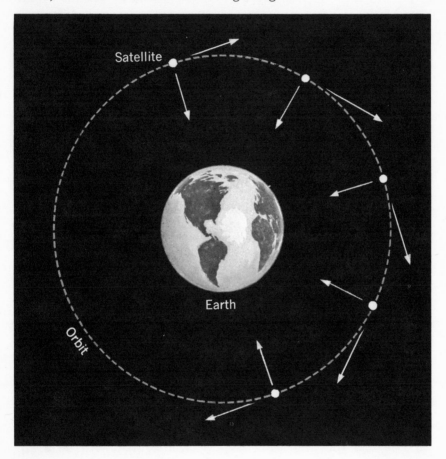

It is perfectly correct, therefore, to say that a satellite is continually falling toward the earth. The same thing is true of the moon. It has been falling toward the earth for several billion years. But it never arrives.

A satellite will keep going forever if it is launched high enough in the sky. A satellite loses energy if the nearest point of its orbit is low enough to encounter air resistance. As a result, it settles still lower in the sky until finally it is burned up by friction against the denser part of the atmosphere.

If a satellite were launched exactly parallel to the earth's surface and at exactly the right speed, its orbit would be a circle. Any deviation in direction or speed will result in an orbit that is an ellipse instead of a circle.

Instead of having a center as a circle does, an ellipse has two points known as the foci. The orbits of the earth and other planets are all ellipses with the sun at one focus.

The term *perigee* has long been used to describe the point at which the moon is nearest to the earth. In Greek, *peri* means "near," and *gee* means "earth."

The word *apogee* refers to the point at which the moon is farthest from the earth. *Apo* is Greek for "away from."

Scientists use *perigee* to refer to a satellite's lowest point, and *apogee* to refer to its highest point.

To put a satellite into space at an altitude of 300 miles above the earth's surface requires a velocity of 17,000 miles an hour. If the launching is perfect, the orbit will be a circle. But if the last stage is given a velocity greater than 17,000 miles an hour, the orbit will become an ellipse with the earth at one focus.

If the last stage of the rocket is 300 miles above the

earth when it puts the satellite into orbit, this altitude will be the perigee of the orbit. Directly opposite will be the point where the satellite is farthest from the earth. This, of course, is the apogee.

As we increase the speed of launching, the apogee will be farther and farther from the earth. We can have a whole family of elliptical orbits, like this:

Of course, if we keep on increasing the speed of our rocket, we finally reach a point where the satellite escapes from the earth's gravitational pull. The velocity of escape, as it is called, is 25,000 miles an hour.

But while the satellite has now escaped from the earth's gravitational pull, it is still subject to the gravitational pull of the sun. As a result, it goes into an orbit around the sun just as the earth is in orbit around the sun.

Scientists usually restrict the name *satellite* to a spacecraft which goes into orbit around the earth. If it goes into orbit around the sun, it is called a *space probe*. The term *lunar probe* is used for one that either goes around the moon and returns to earth or lands on the moon.

To send a probe around the moon, we must give it a velocity less than the velocity of escape. If it is launched with a velocity of 24,800 miles per hour, the apogee of its orbit will be 280,000 miles from the earth. If we time our launching properly, it will go around the moon and return to the earth. The moon's average distance from the earth is approximately 240,000 miles.

This probe will not move with constant velocity. As it travels toward the moon, it will be rising against the gravitational pull of the earth. This will cause it to slow down. The farther it gets from the earth, the more slowly it will move.

However, when it gets within about 40,000 miles of the moon, the moon's gravitational pull will begin to affect it. As a result, it will begin to pick up speed. However, it will still be moving only a few hundred miles per hour as it goes around the moon.

On the return journey, it will begin to pick up speed because the earth's gravitational force is now pulling it back. This will be counteracted to some degree during the first 40,000 miles by the moon's gravitational pull. For the probe, from the standpoint of the moon, is rising against the moon's gravitational force.

However, the probe will continue to gain speed and by the time it gets back to the perigee of its orbit, it will

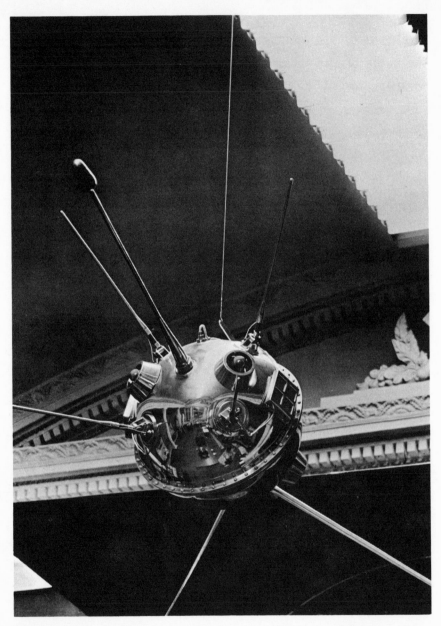

Model of Lunik I, first man-made object to go into orbit around the sun.

again be moving with a velocity of 24,800 miles per hour.

The moon's gravitational pull will make some change in the orbit of the probe, depending upon how close it comes to the moon.

A probe will take about 157 hours to make the trip around the moon and back to earth. Because of its reduced speed near the top of its orbit, it will spend about 50 hours in the neighborhood of the moon.

Lunik III, launched by the Soviet Union on October 4, 1959, went around the moon in this fashion.

If a probe is launched with a velocity greater than the velocity of escape, it will go into orbit around the sun, becoming an artificial planet. Its precise orbit will depend upon both its velocity and the direction in which it is launched.

Man-made planets now in orbit around the sun include the U.S. probes, Pioneer IV and Pioneer V, and the Russian Lunik I and Venus I.

Such space probes will answer many problems about the solar system.

Miniature magnetic tape recorder used in Explorer III.

7. Scientific Tools in Space

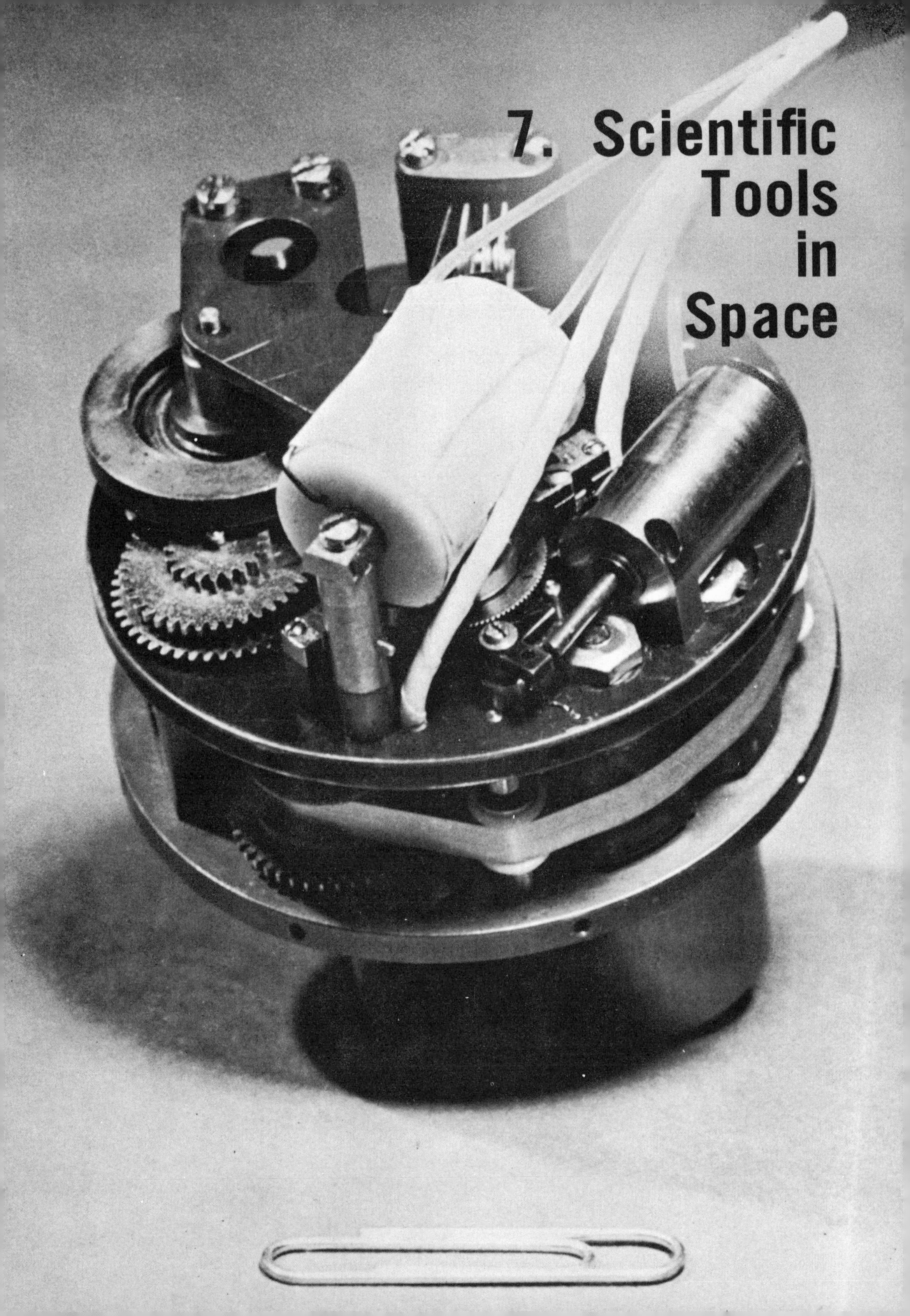

The man-made satellites circling the earth are important scientific tools. They are constantly sending us new information about the nature of the earth, its magnetic field, the atmosphere, outer space, the sun, cosmic rays, and meteors. They also tell us the things we need to know in order to build passenger-carrying space ships.

We live on the bottom of an ocean of air, for the earth's atmosphere is a great sea over our heads. A rocket trip to the moon will begin with a journey through this ocean and will end with a return trip through it.

We must learn how to navigate this aerial sea before we can venture beyond it. We must know more about its winds at high altitudes, the variations in its temperature and density at different levels, the changes in its electrical and chemical behavior.

We must know more about the sun's ultraviolet rays, the cosmic rays, and the constant rain of meteors. On the earth's surface we are protected from these by the dense lower portion of the atmosphere. In a space ship we will no longer have this protection.

More information about the upper atmosphere will be useful for many reasons besides space travel. It will help us to make better weather forecasts. Perhaps the day will come when we can predict weather a year in advance.

Improvements in radio and television will come when we know more about the ways in which radio waves are reflected by the electrified layers of the upper atmosphere.

The smallest satellite in space is Vanguard I. It is only 6 inches in diameter, and it weighs only 3¼ pounds.

It carries no instruments except two radios. One, powered by mercury batteries, became silent after two weeks. The other, drawing its power from solar batteries, is still uttering its shrill beep-beep. Scientists expect that, unless some part wears out, it will continue to operate as long as the satellite remains in orbit—a century or two.

The amazing thing about the instruments carried by many satellites is their small size. Some of these instruments weigh only a few ounces. They are built with all the care and precision of a fine watch.

Almost every satellite has an electronic brain and a magnetic memory as well as a radio voice. Together they form a "telemetering system."

Information collected by the various instruments is stored in the magnetic memory units. Then each record is played back in turn to the radio transmitter, causing variations in the beep-beep of the radio signal. This is done either at the command of the satellite's own electronic brain or in response to a radio command sent from a station on, earth.

Receiving stations in the United States and other parts of the world record the satellite's signals on magnetic tape recorders. The tape in turn is used to produce a visible pattern of jagged lines on film. From the pattern of these lines, the scientists read the information which the satellite collects.

The instruments in the satellites have to be designed so that their readings can be converted into electrical impulses.

For example, an ordinary thermometer would not be useful in outer space. The thermometer used by a satellite is known as a thermistor. It is a tiny metal disk mounted on the outside of the satellite. An electric current is sent through it.

As the temperature goes up or down, the electrical resistance of the disk changes, and so the strength of the current changes. This change in the current is stored in the magnetic memory unit and later broadcast to earth by the radio.

In addition to the temperatures of outer space, scientists wish to know more about the meteors encountered by a satellite. Billions of meteors enter the earth's atmosphere every day. Most of them range in size from dust particles to grains of sand. But some are larger.

One detector is called an erosion gauge. This is a tiny ribbon of metal mounted on the outside of the satellite. An electric current passes through the ribbon. The impact of the meteors wears the ribbon away. The strength of the current grows less and less. This decrease is recorded by the magnetic memory and later broadcast to scientists on the ground.

Another type of detector consists of a little grid of very fine wires. If a meteor hits the grid, it will break the wires, interrupting the electric circuit. If a satellite has a number of these grids, the number of meteors in its neighborhood can be calculated from the life of the grids.

A third method is to place a microphone inside the shell of the satellite. It records the ping of meteors that strike against the satellite.

Scientists also use satellites to obtain information about cosmic rays in outer space. These rays consist of swiftly moving subatomic particles, mostly hydrogen nuclei or protons.

One form of cosmic-ray detector is the Geiger counter. When a cosmic ray goes through it, the ray triggers the release of an electric impulse. Clusters of Geiger counters are used to indicate the direction as well as the strength of the cosmic rays. Similar detectors are used to measure streams of subatomic particles released by the sun.

One of the most important scientific discoveries of recent years was made by the very first U.S. satellite.

Explorer I, launched on January 31, 1958, carried eleven pounds of instruments to make various measurements.

At altitudes of 600 miles or so, its Geiger counters behaved normally, providing an accurate count of the number of cosmic rays encountered each second.

But at altitudes above 1,000 miles, the instruments encountered intense radiations that jammed them.

The same thing happened to the Geiger counters in Explorer III, a satellite very much like Explorer I, which was launched on March 26, 1958.

Dr. James A. Van Allen of the State University of Iowa analyzed the data sent back by these two satellites. He showed that the earth is surrounded by a great belt of intense radiation. It starts at an altitude of 1,400 miles and goes up to 3,400 miles.

The existence of a second belt of intense radiation was revealed by a U.S. space probe, Pioneer III, which was launched on December 6, 1958. This reached an altitude of 63,580 miles above the earth. It revealed that the second belt begins at about 7,000 miles and goes up to about 13,000 miles.

An electronic technician adjusts one of the many antennas used to track satellites.

The two belts have been named the Van Allen belts after Dr. Van Allen. It is now known that they surround the earth like two gigantic doughnuts, one within the other. They lie in the plane of the earth's equator.

The belts consist of subatomic particles that have been trapped by the earth's magnetic field. The outer belt is believed to be composed of electrons hurled out of the sun and trapped as they approached the earth. The inner belt contains both protons and electrons. These are believed to be the product of collisions between incoming cosmic rays with atoms at the top of the earth's atmosphere.

It is highly important to determine quickly the exact orbit of a satellite. This enables scientists to keep in touch with the satellite by radio and to issue commands to it. In addition, a great deal of information can be gained from knowing the exact orbit of each satellite.

The radio and radar stations along the Atlantic Missile Range play a part in this, but they are not sufficient for the purpose. Twelve radio stations have been established in a sort of picket line along the east coast of North America and the west coast of South America. These are known as the Minitrack receiving stations.

The exact determination of satellite orbits is enabling scientists to arrive at a better understanding of the exact shape of the earth and to make better maps of the world.

As antennas were attached to Vanguard II, the gantry was reflected in its shiny surface.

It is possible to calculate the exact position of the center of the earth with reference to the orbit of a satellite. Once this is known, scientists can then calculate how far each radio station is from the center of the earth. From this information, the exact shape of the earth can be determined.

Careful study of the orbit of little Vanguard I has revealed that the earth, in addition to bulging at the equator, is slightly pear-shaped. It is somewhat more pointed in the north and somewhat more rounded in the south.

With the experience gained since 1958, American scientists are now designing more complicated satellites to make more exact measurements of the earth's magnetic field, cosmic rays, and other features of outer space. They are also designing larger satellites which will require bigger rockets to launch them.

Among the space projects planned by NASA scientists are OSO (orbiting solar observatory) and OAO (orbiting astronomical observatory). These will contain telescopes and other equipment for the study of the sun, the planets, and the stars. An observatory in space will not suffer from interference and distortion by the earth's atmosphere. Thus we will learn much more about the planets and the stars.

Large satellites such as these will gradually open the way for manned laboratories and observatories in orbit around the earth.

Testing the television cameras of Tiros II.

8. Weather Satellites

A revolution in weather forecasting is under way. Before long, the weatherman will be able to make more accurate forecasts than ever before, and to make them further in advance.

The revolution was begun by America's first weather-eye satellites, Tiros I, Tiros II, and Tiros III. The name Tiros was taken from the initials of "Television and Infra-Red Observation Satellite."

Peering down from outer space, satellites of this type give scientists pictures of the distribution of the clouds over the face of the earth. The scientists who study the weather, the meteorologists, have long wished for something like this.

Seven "weather eyes," all circling the earth at the same time, could give meteorologists a complete 24-hour-a-day picture of the cloud pattern over the entire earth.

Tiros I was launched on April 1, 1960, with the aid of a three-stage Thor-Able rocket. The satellite was put in a nearly circular orbit at an altitude of approximately 450 miles.

Shaped like a giant hatbox, Tiros I is 42 inches in diameter and 19 inches high. It weighs 270 pounds. Its top and sides are covered with 9,000 tiny solar cells which charge its storage batteries.

Projecting from the bottom of the satellite are the eyes of two television cameras. One is a wide-angle camera to take pictures of an area 800 miles square. The other is a narrow-angle camera with a field 80 miles square.

Four radio antennas jut out at angles from the bottom of the satellite. These transmit the television pictures to earth. There is another antenna on top of the satellite. This receives radio commands sent to the satellite from earth.

The cloud pictures taken by the television cameras are stored on magnetic video tape. They are not transmitted to earth until a command has been received.

When Tiros I went into orbit, it was spinning at the rate of about 136 revolutions per minute. This was too fast to obtain television pictures without blurring. After the satellite was in orbit for 10 minutes, two weights, attached to long cables, were released. As these weights swung outward, they slowed down the spin of the satellite to about 12 revolutions per minute. Then the hooks holding the cables

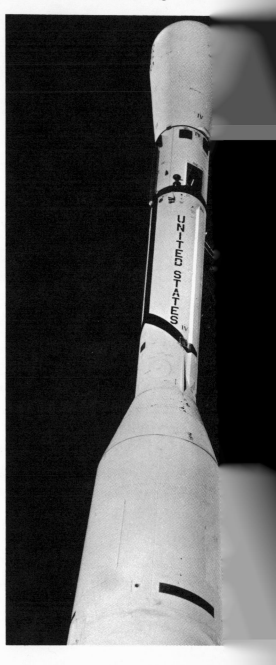

Tiros I was launched from the uppermost stage of a Thor-Able rocket.

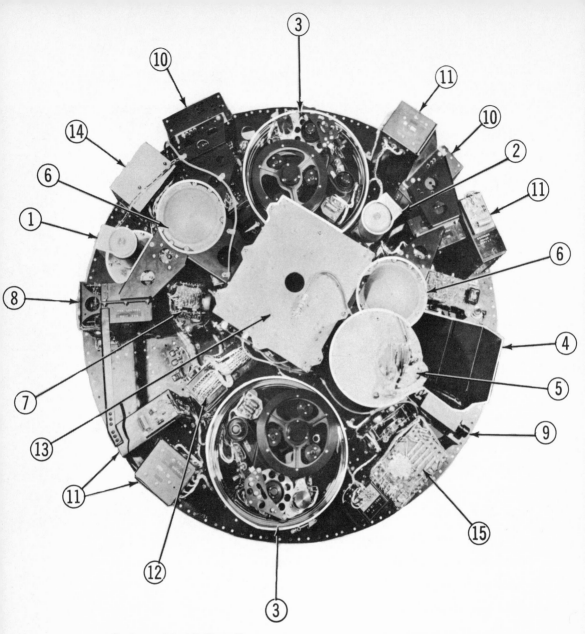

Equipment inside Tiros II

(1) Wide-angle TV camera
(2) Narrow-angle TV camera
(3) Television tape recorders
(4) Infrared system, 5-channel radi-
    ometer
(5) Infrared system electronics
(6) Electronic clocks for timing se-
    quence of operations
(7) Relays for magnetic stabilization
    system controlling satellite's at-
    titude

(8) Control box for electronic sys-
    tems
(9) Infrared horizon scanner
(10) Electronic circuits for cameras
(11) Electronic circuits for TV tape
    recorders
(12) Telemetry switches
(13) Antenna diplexer (covering stor-
    age batteries)
(14) Automatic signal generator
(15) Fuse board and current regulator

to the satellite opened, permitting the cables and weights to separate from the satellite.

By May 31, 1960, the spin of the satellite had slowed down to about nine revolutions per minute. This was a little too slow to keep the satellite stabilized. A radio command fired two small spin rockets on the exterior of the satellite. This caused it to rotate a little faster.

During its active life, Tiros I sent back more than 22,-000 pictures of the clouds. These furnished much new information about the cloud formations associated with large-scale storms. They showed spiral formations connected with large storms which had been previously unsuspected.

Tiros I stopped sending back useful pictures on June 15, 1960, because of breakdowns in its equipment.

Tiros II was launched on November 23, 1960. The satellite is essentially the same size and shape as Tiros I but 10 pounds heavier. In addition to its two television cameras, it contains devices for measuring the amount of heat or infrared radiation received by the earth from the sun and the amount radiated back into space by the earth. This information is expected to be of great assistance to meteorologists in arriving at a better understanding of the weather.

The narrow-angle camera covers an area of 5,625 square miles, while the wide-angle camera covers an area of 562,-000 square miles.

A later satellite, Tiros III, was the first to discover a hurricane from above. On September 10, 1961, the satellite reported that Hurricane Esther was forming in the Atlantic Ocean. Without the information from Tiros III, weathermen would not have known about this dangerous hurricane for several more days.

NASA scientists plan to follow the Tiros satellites with the more advanced Nimbus satellites. With the aid of satellites, the weatherman will some day be able to forecast the weather weeks—or even months—in advance.

Transit III-B with satellite Lofti riding "piggyback." In space the two satellites were separated by a spring mechanism. Lofti tested the transmission of low-frequency radio signals through the ionosphere.

9. Communication Satellites

Before long, you may be able to tune in live television programs from anywhere in the world. Just imagine how thrilling it will be when you can watch the Olympic games or an important international conference on another continent.

The United States opened the way for global television with Project Echo.

Today we can get only local stations on our television sets. This is because the very short radio waves carrying television programs are not reflected back to earth from the ionosphere. They go right through the ionosphere into outer space.

Project Echo made use of a satellite to reflect the waves back to earth. Echo I was launched on August 12, 1960, with a three-stage rocket. Perhaps you watched it cross the sky each night. More conspicuous than any previous satellite, it rivaled the brightest stars.

Echo I was a gigantic balloon, as tall as a 10-story building, made out of plastic only half as thick as the wrapping on a package of cigarets. It was coated with a very thin layer of aluminum. This aluminum coating, which made the satellite look so bright in the sky, reflected the radio waves that were bounced off it.

At launching, the balloon was folded in a container 26½ inches in diameter, in the nose of the rocket. When the rocket reached the desired orbit, the container popped open, tossing the balloon into space.

Inflated to its 100-foot diameter, Echo I dwarfed the men in the foreground and the car in the background.

In outer space, the tiny amount of air trapped in the folded balloon was enough to cause it to unfold. The balloon also contained thirty pounds of a chemical powder which turned to gas as the heat of the sun warmed up the balloon. This supplied enough pressure to inflate the balloon fully. Its orbit was nearly circular, with a perigee of 945 miles and an apogee of 1049 miles. It made one trip

around the earth every 118 minutes.

First, two-way radio telephone conversations were bounced off Echo I. Then a phonograph recording of "America, the Beautiful" was sent across the Atlantic and tuned in by the big radio telescope at Jodrell Bank near Manchester, England.

A picture of President Eisenhower was telecast by a station in Iowa and received in Texas.

Echo I was called a passive communications satellite because it merely reflected the radio waves which hit it.

Courier I-B, launched on October 4, 1960, is an active communications satellite. It is a metallic sphere, 12 feet in diameter, containing 300 pounds of equipment. It stores up radio messages received from ground stations and repeats them either immediately or on radio command. It can receive and transmit 372,500 words during a five-minute pass over a ground station.

Plans are now being made for satellites resembling Echo I which will contain amplifying equipment like that used in the relay towers of the radio and television networks. These will catch the waves reaching them and amplify them before returning them to earth.

Communications satellites will be used not only for television but for world-wide telephone conversations as well.

The transmitter (left) and receiver (right) used for radio telephone conversations via Echo I. The time exposure at the top of the page shows Echo I crossing the sky, tracked by the transmitter—a 60-foot "dish" antenna.

The channels available for transcontinental or transoceanic radio are badly overcrowded and new ones are needed. Experts estimate that it will cost less to employ communications satellites than to lay additional cables across the oceans.

Satellites for communication and for forecasting the weather prove that satellites can be put to practical use. Another group of useful satellites are the Transit satellites.

Each one contains a radio which operates on a frequency that is accurately controlled by a crystal oscillator. A ship at sea or an airplane in the air can check its position more accurately with the aid of such a radio beacon in space than by older methods of navigation.

The development of satellites that serve practical purposes is an important part of the U.S. space program.

Astronaut Shepard awaiting the take-off.

10. Man Into Space

The National Aeronautics and Space Administration took charge of the nation's space program on October 1, 1958. Four days later, it set up a special unit known as the Space Task Group to plan Project Mercury. The purpose of this project was to put American astronauts into outer space.

Scientists and engineers began to design the satellite which would carry the first American into space. Then began a search for astronauts.

The NASA decided that an astronaut must be a military test pilot who had flown jet planes and acquired 1,500 hours or more of flight time. He must be a graduate of a test-pilot school, an engineer, under forty years of age, and not over 5 feet 11 inches tall.

More than a hundred volunteers came forward. The NASA chose thirty-two of them to undergo a series of strenuous tests to determine their physical fitness, mental alertness, emotional balance, and ability to meet the physical and mental strains of space flight.

They were isolated for hours in a dark, soundproof room. They were whirled around in a high-speed centrifuge to determine their ability to withstand the acceleration forces of a rocket take-off. They were tumbled about in a device that tested their sense of equilibrium.

Seven of the group were chosen as the most fit. In April 1959, they began their training as Mercury astronauts.

They returned to the centrifuge to accustom themselves

The centrifuge (above) and training in weightlessness (below).

to the crushing forces that must be endured at take-off.

In the centrifuge, a passenger is whirled around at the end of a pivoted beam. He is subjected to a centrifugal force that becomes greater as the speed of whirling is increased. The force is measured in terms of how much stronger it is than the force of gravity. It is known as 2g, 3g, and so on. At 3g, the rider finds it difficult to lift his arms or legs or head. At 8g, breathing becomes difficult.

Riding on special couches shaped to their exact contours, the Mercury astronauts learned to take up to 20g for very brief periods.

They began training to accustom themselves to the condition known as weightlessness or zero gravity. Originally,

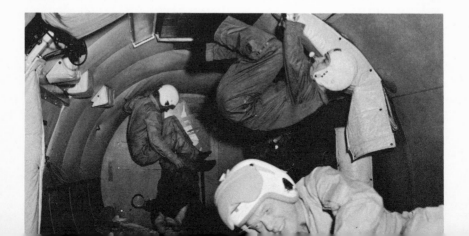

this was known as "free fall," because it resembles the condition encountered in a fall from a high place.

Normally we are aware of our weight because the ground under us supports us and causes us to resist the pull of the earth's gravity. In a free fall—as in a delayed parachute jump—the individual is falling freely with acceleration due to the force of gravity. As a result, he experiences the sensation of weightlessness.

This same sensation is experienced in a rocket once it is coasting, whether it is moving away from the earth's surface or toward it. The reason is that, in either case, the rocket is responding to the full effect of gravity.

Weightlessness can be achieved briefly in an airplane. The pilot puts the plane into a dive to increase its speed and then pulls up into a steep climb. As the plane rises, he decreases the power until the plane almost stalls. Then, as the plane descends, he increases the power. As a result, the plane moves in a curved path like that of a ball tossed by one person to another.

During this time, the pilot and his passengers experience weightlessness. Passengers find themselves floating around in the cabin of the plane. If an object is released, it does not fall to the floor of the cabin but remains suspended in space.

The Mercury astronauts, while undergoing weightlessness, practiced drinking orange juice and soup from squeeze bottles.

One of the most startling training devices for astronauts is the Multiple Axis Space Test Inertia Facility. This consists of a chair mounted in the center of an elaborate system of circular steel frames. Jets of nitrogen gas released from tanks attached to the framework make the chair twist and roll and turn somersaults.

The astronaut is strapped securely into the chair. Then an engineer starts the chair on its dizzy gyrations. The astronaut counters its wild motions with the aid of a control stick. The purpose of the device is to train him for the task of controlling his spacecraft in case of emergency.

The satellite used for the first American flights into space is known as the Mercury capsule. It has an outer shell of heat-resistant cobalt and an inner shell of titanium. Insulation between the two shells protects the passenger from heat, cold, and noise.

Shaped like a gigantic television image tube, the capsule is 9½ feet long and 6 feet across at its broad end. It weighs about 1½ tons.

Wearing an air-conditioned pressure suit, the astronaut is strapped into a fiberglas chair. There is a different chair for each astronaut.

At the large end of the capsule there is a heat shield that makes it possible for the capsule to re-enter the atmosphere from outer space. At the small end, there are parachutes that open at the proper time to permit the capsule to descend gently to the surface of the Atlantic.

The equipment of the capsule is so complex that it contains seven miles of electrical wiring. All the controls can be operated in three ways—automatically, or by radio command from the ground, or by the astronaut himself.

The Mercury capsule was subjected to numerous tests before the first astronaut made a flight in it. In a final test, on January 31, 1961, a 37-pound chimpanzee, named Ham, was given a ride over the Atlantic Missile Range. His flight, from Cape Canaveral to the landing on the ocean, lasted 18 minutes. The capsule was picked up from the water by a Navy helicopter.

Ham was found to be in excellent condition. The same evening he ate an apple, half an orange, and a small wedge

Mockup of a Mercury capsule and escape rocket.

of lettuce, washed down by a big drink of water.

Encouraged by the success of this test, officials of the NASA scheduled the first suborbital flight by a Mercury astronaut. Commander Alan B. Shepard, Jr., was chosen to make the first flight. The historic event took place on May 5, 1961.

The Mercury capsule, which had been named the Freedom 7, was mounted on top of a Redstone rocket at Cape Canaveral with its broad end against the top of the rocket. This meant that at take-off Commander Shepard would be lying on his back with his knees up. Tests had shown that this was the best position in which to take the crushing force of the take-off.

Rising above the capsule there was a little tower of steel girders ending in a solid-fuel rocket. This was the escape rocket. If anything

On his return from space, Ham reached for an apple.

had gone wrong during the launching, the capsule could have been separated from the Redstone and the escape rocket ignited. Then the escape rocket and its little tower would have separated from the capsule and the parachute would have opened, permitting the capsule to descend gently.

Shepard was awakened at 1:05 A.M. on the morning of

his flight. He ate a breakfast of filet mignon wrapped in bacon, two poached eggs, dry toast with jelly, and orange juice. After breakfast he was given a careful physical examination by the project physician.

Then a number of electrodes were taped to his body. When he entered the Mercury capsule, these would be connected to instruments which would record his heart beat, respiration, and body temperature and transmit this information back by radio.

Wearing his silver-colored pressure suit, he arrived at the launching pad at 4:27 A.M. The Redstone rocket, surrounded by the huge gantry, gleamed in the light of a battery of searchlights. A yellow half-moon shone in the sky overhead. At 5:15 A.M., Shepard entered the elevator of the gantry. It took him to the level of the capsule. A few minutes later, he climbed into it.

At 5:20, the countdown stood at T-minus-100-minutes. Shepard was scheduled to begin his historic flight in just 100 minutes. The breaking dawn began to tint the clouds on the eastern horizon with pink.

The hatch on the capsule was closed at 6:10. Shepard was now sealed in the capsule for his flight down the Atlantic Missile Range.

Slowly, the gantry crane moved away, leaving the Redstone rocket with its Mercury capsule standing alone in the sunlight.

A mobile boom crane, resembling those used by tree-

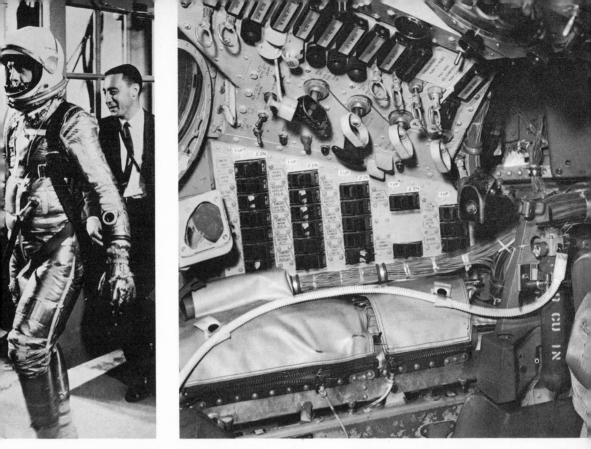

Left: Astronaut Shepard en route to the rocket, accompanied by Astronaut Grissom. Right: Part of Shepard's control panel.

trimmers and nicknamed the "cherry picker," moved into place near the rocket. In the event of any emergency before the rocket was fired, this would enable Shepard to leave the capsule quickly.

Grey clouds began to cover the sky at 7 A.M., and it was decided to hold the countdown until a new weather report was obtained. Then trouble developed in one of the electronic devices in the rocket. The cherry picker moved away and the big gantry was brought back over the launching pad.

Shepard remained sealed in the capsule. Two air-conditioning lines continued to keep it cool.

At 8:40 the gantry was pulled back, the "cherry picker" brought forward, and the countdown resumed at T-minus-35-minutes. At 9:00 another hold was ordered to check on a computer. The countdown was resumed 17 minutes later, but at 9:30 another hold was ordered to check a pressure gauge. The trouble was cleared up in a minute and the countdown was resumed.

Shepard had been lying inside the Mercury capsule for more than four hours. But the record of his heartbeat and respiration continued steady.

The last two minutes of the countdown proceeded without incident. Tension grew greater and greater in the blockhouse. At 13 seconds after 9:34 A.M., the Redstone ignited and began to lift off the launching pad, its flaming tail looking pale in the sunlight.

Shepard had been instructed to read the dials on the instrument panel of the capsule and to call them out. His voice came clearly, 30 seconds after take-off: "This is Freedom 7. The fuel is go." By "go," Shepard meant that the rocket was operating properly.

As the rocket gathered speed, Shepard experienced a force of acceleration that quickly increased to 5g. The Redstone exhausted its fuel 2 minutes and 22 seconds after the take-off. The rocket was now over the Atlantic Ocean at an altitude of 37 miles and beginning to tilt toward the east-southeast.

Shepard's take-off, May 5, 1961.

Ten seconds later, the Mercury capsule was automatically separated from the Redstone. The escape rocket and its tower were also cut loose. The Mercury capsule was now in free flight and Shepard experienced weightlessness.

Next the capsule automatically turned so that Shepard was riding with his back to the direction of flight.

At 9:38, Shepard called out, "A-Okay. Switching to manual pitch." This was notice that Shepard was taking over the piloting of the Mercury capsule himself instead of depending upon the automatic controls. The expression "A-Okay" meant "All O.K."

Half a minute later, viewing the earth through the capsule's periscope, Shepard exclaimed, "What a beautiful sight!"

Next Shepard put his space ship through a series of prescribed maneuvers, causing it to pitch up and down, to rock from side to side, and to roll on its axis. This was done by releasing jets of hydrogen peroxide from a series of nozzles.

At 9:39, the Mercury capsule was at the high point of the flight, 115 miles above the Atlantic. Shepard now put the capsule into position for the descent and fired the three retro rockets in succession.

At 9:42 the capsule re-entered the denser portion of the earth's atmosphere. As air resistance began to slow the capsule, Shepard no longer experienced weightlessness. Instead, he began to feel the gradually increasing force of deceleration. This rose to 10g as the capsule slowed from 4500 miles an hour to 341 miles an hour.

A minute later, the force of deceleration had let up. At 9:44, when the capsule was down to about 30,000 feet, the small stabilizing parachute opened up. Then the big parachute opened. The capsule had now descended to 7,000 feet.

It landed on the water at 9:49, just 302 miles from Cape Canaveral. Shepard had completed his 15-minute ride through space.

Four minutes later, he climbed out of the capsule and was picked up by a Navy helicopter.

"Boy, what a ride," he told the crew, as the helicopter headed for the flight deck of the airplane carrier *Lake Champlain*.

Three days later Shepard was given a hero's welcome in the city of Washington. He received the NASA Distinguished Service Medal from the President in a ceremony at the White House.

Recovery of Commander Shepard by helicopter.

A second flight over the Atlantic Missile Range was made by Captain Virgil I. Grissom on July 21, 1961. He rode in the Liberty Bell 7, a Mercury capsule which was also boosted into space by a Redstone rocket.

The third Mercury astronaut to venture into space and

the first American to orbit the earth was Lieutenant Colonel John H. Glenn, Jr. He made three circuits around the earth in the Friendship 7, a Mercury capsule, on February 20, 1962. An Atlas rocket launched the capsule.

Glenn took off from Cape Canaveral at 6:03 A.M. He traveled about 81,000 miles in 4 hours and 56 minutes at a speed of 17,545 miles an hour. His altitude ranged from 100 to 160 miles. He kept in communication with the 18 radio stations of the worldwide tracking system as he circled the earth. His voice was confident and jubilant.

At 2:43 P.M., the capsule landed safely on the Atlantic Ocean near Grand Turk Island in the Bahamas, about 800 miles southeast of Cape Canaveral. Twenty-one minutes later the capsule was lifted out of the water by the U.S. destroyer *Noa*.

In 1959, Russian astronauts—called cosmonauts—had begun training for flights into space.

Later the Soviet Union launched several spacecraft, which the Russians referred to as cosmic space ships or Sputnik ships. Each weighed about five tons and contained a cabin capable of keeping a man alive in space. Some contained dummy space men. Some carried dogs and other animals.

One of the Russian spacecraft made a successful trip on March 25, 1961. Apparently the Russian scientists were now satisfied that the time had come to put their first cosmonaut into orbit.

The start of John Glenn's orbital flight, February 20, 1962. The Atlas rocket has just risen from its launching pad at Cape Canaveral.

Major Yuri Gagarin was launched into space at 9:07 A.M. on April 12, 1961. His ship was called the Vostok. It orbited the earth once, reaching a maximum altitude of 188 miles and traveling at a speed of more than 17,000 miles an hour. It landed near the village of Smelovka in the Saratov region at 10:55 A.M. Major Gagarin had been aloft for 108 minutes.

During his flight, Gagarin talked by radio with Russian ground stations. Tape recordings of these conversations were later broadcast. The cosmonaut reported that he felt fine, that weightlessness was not troubling him, and that he could see the earth clearly from his space ship.

On his return he said that he had had no difficulty in eating jelly and drinking water from squeeze bottles. He said that he floated in mid-air in the space ship and that other objects were swimming about him. However, he had no trouble writing in his notebook, although his arms felt weightless.

"The day side of the earth was clearly visible," he said. "The coasts of continents, islands, big rivers, big surfaces of water, and structural features were clearly distinguishable.

"I saw for the first time with my eyes the earth's spherical shape. You can see its curvature when looking to the horizon. It is possible to see the remarkably colorful change from the light surface of the earth to the completely black sky in which one can see the stars. This dividing line is very thin, just like a belt of film surrounding the earth's sphere. It is of soft light blue color and the entire transition from blue to black is most smooth and beautiful."

Four months later another Russian major, Gherman Titov, undertook the longest journey any man had ever made. Orbiting the earth 17½ times in a space ship, he traveled 435,000 miles before returning safely to the ground.

Other approaches have also been made to the problem of manned flight into space. One of these is the X-15 program.

The X-15 is a needle-nosed, stub-winged craft which has been described as half plane and half rocket ship. It weighs 15 tons.

It is carried to an altitude of eight miles, suspended just below the wing of a big B-52 bomber.

The pilot takes his place in the rocket plane before the take-off. Wearing a pressurized space suit, he straps himself into the cockpit and closes the canopy overhead.

When he gives the signal, the big bomber drops the X-15 and quickly banks out of the way. The pilot starts the rocket motor at once.

Eventually, it is hoped that the X-15 can be flown to an altitude of 100 miles.

Bringing the X-15 back from such an altitude will be an extremely difficult task. As the plane returns to the denser portion of the atmosphere, the front edge of its wings will grow red hot.

Scientists are certain that much can be learned from the X-15 that will eventually be useful in bringing space ships back from outer space.

Some existing and future rockets, showing comparative sizes. Top row, left to right: Atlas, Atlas-Able, Atlas-Agena, and Centaur. Bottom row, left to right: Juno, Thor, Saturn, and Nova.

11. Bigger Boosters

The future of space exploration depends upon the development of bigger and more powerful rockets capable of putting bigger and more complex spacecraft into orbit. The scientists and engineers refer to the rockets as "boosters," while the satellite or space probe is known as the "payload."

The National Aeronautics and Space Administration has planned a new series of large rockets.

One of these is the Centaur. Its first stage will be an Atlas, originally designed for an inter-continental ballistic missile. The second stage will be a new high-energy rocket employing liquid hydrogen and liquid oxygen. This will be very much more powerful than any of the upper stages now in use and will make it possible to put a four-ton payload into orbit.

The next rocket under development by the NASA is a giant. The exploration of space will enter a new phase when this rocket, known as the Saturn, puts its first payload into orbit. It will make possible the detailed exploration of the moon.

Following static tests of the first stage of the Saturn at the Marshall Space Flight Center at Huntsville, Alabama, it was sent by barge to Cape Canaveral. The first stage stands 80 feet high and is 22 feet in diameter. It is almost as tall as the three-stage launching rockets now in use, and it is much bigger around. Actually it is a cluster of eight rocket motors, each one an improved and simplified version of the Jupiter. The eight together have a thrust of 1,500,000 pounds.

The completed Saturn C-1 will have three stages. The second stage will itself be a cluster of four rocket motors. These upper stages will be high-energy rockets employing liquid hydrogen and liquid oxygen.

The Saturn C-2 will be even larger and will probably be able to send a three-man Apollo space ship around the moon. A still larger Saturn C-3 is also planned.

Huge as the Saturn is, it will be dwarfed by the next super-giant booster planned by the NASA. This will be known as the Nova.

The Nova's first stage will consist of a cluster of eight F-1 rocket motors, each as powerful as all eight of the Saturn's first stage. Each of the Nova's eight motors will have a thrust of 1,500,000 pounds, making a total thrust of 12,000,000 pounds.

A full-scale testing version of the Saturn C-1 (rear) dwarfs the Juno II (left) and the Mercury-Redstone (foreground).

A technician working with one of the Saturn's eight H-1 engines. Behind it is a full-scale model of an F-1 engine, eight times as powerful, to be used in later Saturn and in Nova rockets.

The Nova's second stage may consist of four high-energy rocket motors using liquid hydrogen and liquid oxygen. Other stages would be mounted on top of this one. The Nova may tower to a height of 360 feet—one quarter the height of the Empire State Building. It will have sufficient power to land an expedition on the moon.

The NASA is also studying the use of atomic energy in rockets. A rocket using atomic energy would be much more powerful than one using chemical fuels. As a result, it would be able to boost bigger payloads into space.

Instead of a combustion chamber, an atomic rocket will contain a nuclear reactor. The rocket will need only one gas. This will not be burned. It will be heated to high temperature in the reactor and then ejected, unchanged, from the nozzle of the rocket.

A nuclear reactor can reach much higher temperature than can be obtained by the combustion of chemical fuels. In addition, an atomic rocket can use either hydrogen or helium as the propellant. These are the two lightest gases in existence.

For both of these reasons, the train of gas will leave the atomic rocket at much greater speed than can be attained with chemical fuels. The performance of a rocket depends upon the speed with which the train of gas is ejected from it. Consequently, the atomic rocket will be superior.

However, there are many technical difficulties that must be overcome in the design of an atomic rocket. One is to find suitable materials from which to build the rocket and its reactor. The higher the temperature of the reactor, the more difficult it is to find suitable materials.

A research program, known as Project Rover, has been launched jointly by the National Aeronautics and Space Administration and by the Atomic Energy Commission (AEC).

Scientists of the AEC are working on the reactor. The rest of the rocket will be designed by the scientists of the NASA. Several experimental reactors have been tested in Nevada at the AEC testing grounds.

Probably the first atomic rockets will be fairly small ones, used for one or more of the upper stages of big multi-stage rockets. It will be some years before an atomic rocket big enough to serve as the first stage can be developed.

It is probable that the first use of an atomic rocket will be as the third stage of a Saturn.

It is estimated that a Saturn with an atomic third stage will be able to put twice as heavy a payload into space as one with a chemical third stage.

Each improvement in rockets will make it possible to put bigger and better satellites and space probes, both unmanned and manned, into orbit. In this fashion, our knowledge of the universe will increase as rockets grow bigger.

A proposed design for Apollo manned spacecraft.

12. Exploring the Moon

Once the first satellites had been put in orbit around the earth, scientists turned their attention to the moon.

The first man-made object to reach the moon was Lunik II, the lunar probe shot into space by the Russians on September 12, 1959. It landed on the moon the next day, having taken about 35 hours for the journey.

Lunik II weighed 858 pounds. Its launching was a scientific achievement of the first magnitude. To hit the moon, Lunik II had to be aimed with the greatest of accuracy.

When the probe was 100,000 miles from the earth, it ejected a cloud of luminous sodium vapor. This was photographed by Russian scientists but could not be seen from the United States.

Scientists calculated that Lunik II made a crater in the moon's surface about 100 feet in diameter. However, it is impossible to identify so tiny a crater among the thousands of other tiny craterlets on the surface of the moon.

On October 4, 1959, Russia sent Lunik III into an elliptical orbit that swept around the moon. It took the first photographs of the other side of the moon.

Lunik III weighed 614 pounds. It contained two cameras. Equipment in Lunik III removed the films from the cameras, developed the films, and then transferred them to a television transmitter which sent them back to earth where they were received by Russian stations.

When launched, Lunik III was spinning rapidly. On October 7, as it swept around the moon, jets of gas were

Model of Lunik III (left), which took the first photographs of the far side of the moon (right).

released from it. These slowed down the spin. The photographs of the moon were taken during the next 40 minutes, while Lunik III was approximately 40,000 miles from the moon.

The photographs are not very clear. They are about as good as the very first pictures of the moon taken in 1850 when photography was still in its infancy. They show that the other side of the moon is mostly mountainous with very few of the great flat plains known as maria.

Astronomers kept track of Lunik III until its radio went dead. It probably re-entered the earth's atmosphere and burned up like a meteor.

The NASA has planned an elaborate program for the exploration of the moon. The program will begin with unmanned lunar probes, known as Project Ranger.

The first Ranger probes will be equipped with retro rockets which will change their path when they reach the lunar neighborhood. As a result, they will go into orbit around the moon. Because they will remain in orbit around the moon, they will tell us very much more about the moon than a lunar probe which merely swings around the moon and returns to earth.

These probes will be equipped with television cameras. It is expected that they will send back better pictures of the hidden side of the moon than the first ones taken by Lunik III.

Next, Ranger probes will crash on the lunar surface just as Lunik II did. These probes will be equipped with television cameras to send back pictures of the lunar surface up to the moment of impact.

Just before they hit the moon, they will release small capsules carrying scientific instruments. Retro rockets will slow up these capsules so that they will make a safe, although rough, landing on the lunar surface.

The capsules will also contain radio transmitters so that the data collected by their instruments can be sent back to earth. It is planned to put a seismograph in the first capsule.

Scientists are certain that there are lunar tremors corresponding to our earthquake waves. Just as the terrestrial waves tell us much about the composition and structure of the earth's interior, so a seismograph on the moon will reveal many secrets of the moon's interior.

The probes which release the capsules will themselves be

destroyed when they crash into the surface of the moon. The NASA scientists speak of this as a "hard" landing.

As the next step in the exploration of the moon, the scientists are planning lunar probes which will make "soft" landings. By this they refer to spacecraft that will land gently and safely on the lunar surface. Such a probe will need very elaborate automatic controls to fire its retro rockets at the right time and guide it to a safe landing.

One design for such a lunar probe has a framework around it like a camera tripod. The probe will settle down on the lunar surface on these legs.

The probe has been given the name of Surveyor. A Centaur booster will be required to get the Surveyor to the moon.

When the Saturn boosters are ready for use, bigger probes will be

Full-scale mockup of Surveyor, soft-landing lunar-exploration vehicle.

landed on the moon. These have been named the Prospectors. It is planned to have one of these bigger probes carry a mobile robot which will be capable of moving about on wheels over an area with a radius of 50 miles. Such a mobile unit will be able to send back a great deal more information about the moon than a stationary Prospector.

Later, as part of Project Apollo, the NASA plans to send a party of three astronauts around the moon in a space ship. There will be no attempt to land on the moon.

Various designs for such a space ship are being studied. One ship under study would have two sections. The lower section, containing comfortable living quarters as well as most of the scientific equipment, will be large.

The upper section will be small and will be designed to permit re-entry into the earth's atmosphere and safe landing on the surface of the earth. When the space ship nears the earth, the astronauts will take their places in the upper section. This will then separate from the lower section. The lower section will burn up like a meteor in the earth's atmosphere, but the upper section will make a safe landing.

Two methods of bringing the upper section to earth are under study. One is to use parachutes. The other is to have it equipped with stubby wings so that it can glide to earth like the X-15.

When the first party of explorers lands on the moon, a 50-ton space ship will be needed to get them there and back to earth again.

Two ways of getting to the moon in a direct flight from the surface of the earth are under study. The first method would make use of a super-giant Nova with six stages.

The first three stages will be needed to launch the last three stages and the space ship with sufficient speed to reach the moon. Each of these first three stages will separate from the assembly as it uses up its fuel.

When the space ship has coasted to the neighborhood of the moon, the pilot will fire the fourth stage. This will change the path of the space ship into an orbit around the moon.

The pilot will permit the ship to go around the moon several times until he has decided upon the best landing place. He will then use the control jets to make the ship roll around so that the fifth stage points forward.

Then he will fire the fifth stage. Its jet will oppose the forward motion of the ship and act as a braking rocket or retro rocket. As the ship slows down, it will circle the moon several times, coming lower and lower each time.

Landing on the moon will require a great deal of care. The space ship will have a number of legs like those of a camera tripod. The pilot will bring the ship down very gently, finally bringing it to rest on its legs. It will then be in a position to take off for the return journey.

When it is time to return to earth, the fifth stage will be disconnected. It will serve merely as a launching platform and will be left behind on the moon.

The space ship will take off when the pilot fires the sixth stage. This will be sufficient to get the space ship off the surface of the moon because the pull of the moon's gravity is only one-sixth as strong as that of the earth. And the moon has no atmosphere to slow up the ship.

The space ship will have a small upper section. As they

near the earth, the astronauts will take their places in it. It will separate from the rest of the ship and the burnt-out sixth stage, and will then re-enter the earth's atmosphere and glide to a landing.

The second method under study for landing a party on the moon would make use of what are known as "rendez-vous and refueling techniques." This will be similar to present methods of using a tanker plane to refuel a jet plane in the air. It will require the use of three giant rockets. The upper stages of one of them will be equipped to make the journey to the moon and back. Those of the other two will be the fuel carriers.

The three rockets, each under the control of a pilot, will be put into the same orbit, 150 miles or so above the surface of the earth. They will then be brought side by side. The two fuel carriers will transfer their fuel to the lunar rocket by means of hose connections and return to earth. The lunar rocket will then restart its motors and take off for the moon.

One suggestion for a 16-ton space station to be used as an earth-orbiting laboratory.

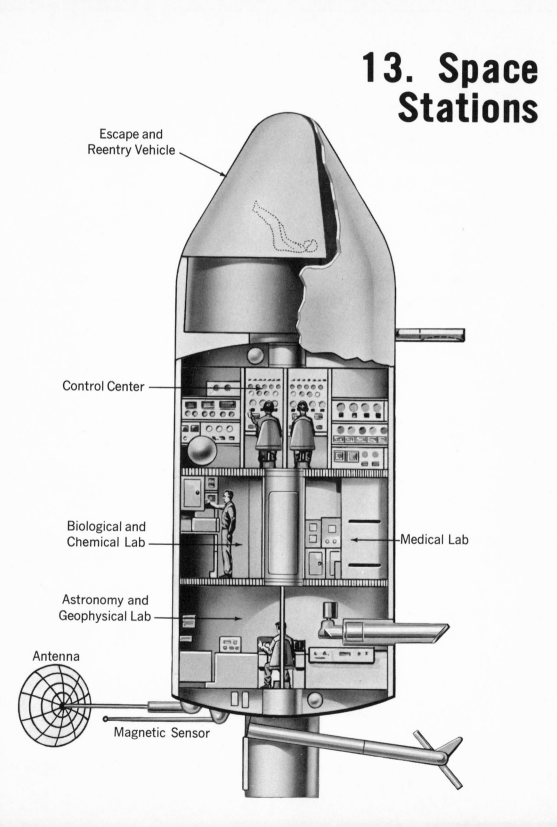

13. Space Stations

Escape and Reentry Vehicle

Control Center

Biological and Chemical Lab

Medical Lab

Astronomy and Geophysical Lab

Antenna

Magnetic Sensor

Even though the first space ship to the moon will probably take off directly from the surface of the earth, scientists want to build space stations.

The first space stations will be small scientific laboratories equipped with telescopes and Geiger counters and other apparatus for studying the sun, the stars, cosmic rays, and the other wonders of the universe.

Bigger space stations will simplify the problems of space travel. They will be the "shipyards" where space ships are built. This will make possible bigger space ships than can be boosted into orbit from the surface of the earth.

A big space station will also serve as a terminal for these ships. Returning from the moon or Mars, the space ships will leave their passengers at the station. Transport rockets will then take them back to the surface of the earth.

The NASA's first small space station may be built on the surface of the earth and boosted into orbit with a Saturn rocket.

Eventually, however, space stations will be built in space in an orbit high above the top of the atmosphere at an altitude of 500 miles or more.

For the construction of such a space station, transport rockets will be needed. They must be capable of going up to such altitudes and returning safely to the surface of the earth.

Materials brought up by these transport rockets will be dumped into space. The engineers and technicians, wearing suitable space suits, will calmly step out of the rockets into space.

Do you have visions of men and material falling to earth, descending in great arcs and burning up like meteors in the dense lower regions of the atmosphere?

This will not happen. When a transport rocket reaches an altitude of 500 miles, the pilot will put it into an orbit like a satellite. If he shuts off the rocket's engines, it will continue in orbit as long as desired.

If a load of steel girders is dumped out of the rocket, it will continue to circle the earth in the same orbit with the rocket. The same thing will happen to the engineer who steps out of the rocket in his space suit.

The men who step out into space will not have any sensation of moving at great speed. Although the earth is going around the sun at 18½ miles a second, you and I do not have any sensation of moving through space.

A number of plans are being studied for the design of space stations. It has even been suggested that one could be built out of light plastic materials with walls of nylon. Such a station could be inflated in outer space, like the satellite Echo I. There is some question, however, as to what meteors might do to a space station of such light construction.

One way of building a space station will be to send up several transport rockets and then bolt them together to make a single structure.

One of the best-known plans for a space station is the one put forward by Dr. Wernher von Braun. His design looks like a big wheel. The main portion of the station is the rim of the wheel. There is a small central structure at the hub of the wheel and corridors that run like spokes from the hub to the rim.

He has suggested that the wheel be made to rotate as it goes around its orbit. Centrifugal force would then take the place of gravity, and the scientists and engineers in the station would not experience the sensation of weightlessness. Such a station might be as much as 250 feet in diameter. It would contain machine shops and scientific laboratories as well as living quarters for scientists and engineers.

Building a space station will not be easy. It calls for the solution of many problems. One of the first is to design space suits that will enable engineers and technicians to step out into space.

These suits will have to be made of metal or plastic, and they will have to be pressurized. Each man will also have to carry his own oxygen supply.

Engineers and mechanics who assemble the space stations will want ropes or cables to anchor them to their work. This is not because of any fear of falling, but to keep them from drifting away. The largest steel girder will be weightless as it goes around in orbit. It will be no trick at all for a man to push such a girder around. But once it starts moving in a given direction, it will continue to drift away

Proposed form of an orbital space laboratory that would spin to simulate gravity.

unless stopped. That is why anchor ropes will be needed to keep men and material together.

It is possible that small "space taxis" will be developed for getting around during the construction job. These will need very little rocket power.

Workmen will have to get used to working in space. On the surface of the earth, the sunlight is scattered in all directions by the molecules of air. But in space the sunlit side of an object will be intensely bright. The opposite side will be lost in blackness. These peculiar lighting effects will make it difficult for the workmen who are putting the space station together.

The men will also be bothered by extremes of temperature. An object in the sunlight will become extremely hot, while one in shadow will be extremely cold.

It will be fascinating to visit a space station. The sky around you will be black, with both the sun and the stars shining at the same time. The stars will be sharper and clearer than you have ever seen them. They will not twinkle, because the twinkling we see from earth is caused by movements of our atmosphere.

The sun will be much brighter. Extending a great distance out from its edge will be a silvery halo. This is the sun's corona, a feature seen from earth only during a total eclipse of the sun or with the aid of special instruments.

You will see the earth as a great globe surrounded by a blue haze. With the aid of binoculars or a small telescope, you will have no difficulty in making out rivers and mountains, coastlines and oceans.

Now you feel as though the earth is standing still while the sun moves across the heavens from sunrise to sunset. When you visit a space station, you will have the sensation that the station is standing still—and that the earth is moving around you.

The view shortly before a landing on the moon.

14. A Trip to the Moon

Some day, perhaps, you will make a trip to the moon. At the launching field, an elevator will take you up one of the towers of the gantry crane. You will cross the gangplank that takes you into the cabin of the third stage of the transport rocket.

When all the passengers are in, the doors of the cabin will be tightly closed and the air-conditioning apparatus will be turned on. Then the gantry crane will move out of the way.

The command pilot will check his instruments and then give the signal for the take-off. Your seat and those of the other passengers will be tipped back to form beds. There will be a tremendous roar as the motors of the first stage ignite. As the rocket rises into the air, you will feel a pressure of about 2g.

But in a couple of minutes, the motors will have consumed their fuel and now you will feel weightless. Looking out of the portholes, you will see the earth far below and you will be able to recognize that it is a globe. As you rise, the sky will get less and less blue. Finally, it will be black and you will see the stars as well as the sun.

You will feel an increase in "g" when the motors of the second stage are fired and again when the third-stage motors are ignited.

Arriving at the space station, you will transfer from the cabin of your rocket to the station through an air lock. After dinner in the station, you will go through the air lock once more, this time to take your place in the cabin of the lunar ship. You will be on your way to the moon.

As the hours go by, the moon will grow in size and brightness. Soon you have such a view of the moon as you can get on earth with the aid of a good pair of prism binoculars or a small telescope.

Now you see a series of large dark areas on the surface of the moon. You also see the great ranges of mountains that surround these areas and the wild profusion of large and small craters that dot the whole visible surface of the moon.

This was the way the moon looked to Galileo when he turned his first little telescope upon its silvery disk in the year 1610. He thought the dark areas were oceans and so he called them *maria,* the Latin word for "seas." We know today that the moon has neither air nor water, and that what Galileo thought were seas are only great flat plains.

Astronomers have been making maps of the moon since the time of Galileo, and the navigator of the space ship has some of the more recent lunar maps with him.

When you are only 200 miles from the moon, the pilot puts the space ship into a circular orbit around the moon. Now you have a good view of it.

Some of the maria are very large and nearly circular in shape. Mare Imbrium is about 700 miles in diameter. Mare Serenitatis is 430 miles in diameter.

There are ten great mountain ranges on the face of the

moon which we see from earth. These have been named after mountain ranges on earth. So we speak of the Lunar Alps, the Lunar Apennines, and so on. These mountain ranges are extremely rugged and have many tall peaks.

The scene which greets your eyes as the space ship swings around the moon is very different from any you have ever seen on earth.

The most startling features are the craters. These are everywhere. They range in size from very small ones, just barely visible at your altitude of 200 miles, to some more than 100 miles in diameter.

The lunar map-makers named most of the craters after the astronomers of their day. We find craters named Copernicus, Tycho, Kepler, and so on. The largest crater on the moon is named Clavius. It is 146 miles in diameter. There are about 32,000 craters on the face of the moon which is turned toward us. The Russians have named some of the craters on the far side of the moon. These include Tsiolkovsky crater and Lomonosov crater.

Many of the craters are flat plains walled in by rings of mountains. In general, the floor of a crater is lower than the nearby lunar surface, but some of the craters appear to be partially filled with what is either lava or dust. Other craters have saucer-shaped interiors while yet others have mountain peaks rising from their centers.

The rougher areas of the moon's surface are covered with a confused hodgepodge of craters. There are big ones and

Circling the moon, you would see a hodgepodge of large and small craters.

little ones. There are craters within craters and craters that have broken through the walls of other craters.

From the space ship, you see other strange and interesting features of the moon's surface. There are long, straight cliffs, some of them more than fifty miles long. They are thought to have resulted from the settling of large blocks of the moon's surface.

You also see deep cracks in the moon's surface. These are known as rills and sometimes extend for 90 or 100 miles.

A very strange feature are the light-colored streaks extending in all directions from some of the larger craters. Astronomers call them rays. They run over mountains and valleys in almost straight lines.

After circling the moon a number of times, the pilot decides to spiral downward and finally to land the ship gently on one of the maria. You cannot leave the ship until you have donned a space suit.

However beautiful the moon may appear from earth, it is a dangerous and inhospitable place to visit. There is neither air nor water on the moon. The towering mountains are bare rock. There are no rushing mountain streams, no forests of pine and spruce, no carpets of grass.

The direct rays of the sun beat down upon the lunar surface. There is no blanket of air to protect you from them.

Because the moon turns so slowly on its axis, making

one revolution in the same time that it goes once around the earth, any given spot on the moon has approximately two weeks of sunlight, followed by two weeks of darkness.

During the long lunar day, the temperature rises until it is the temperature of boiling water, 212 degrees Fahrenheit. During the long lunar night, the temperature falls until it is 243 degrees below zero.

Parts of the surface of the moon are covered with a layer of pulverized rock and dust. This makes it extremely difficult to get about, since the dust fills the ruts and cracks. You must be extremely careful, for some of the cracks may be very deep and in places the dust may hide sharp ridges and spikes of rock.

However, the fact that the moon's force of gravity is so small is a help. It is only one-sixth of what the force of gravity is on earth. Consequently, you find that you can leap many feet up without any difficulty.

There is a constant rain of meteors upon the surface of the moon. Much of the layer of pulverized rock on the lunar surface is the result of this bombardment.

When you are ready to go home, you will re-enter the space ship. The pilot will start the engine of the space ship and head back for the space station. Once again, you will enter the space station through an air lock. You will have dinner again in the station. Then you will enter a transport ship that will take you back to the surface of the earth.

Dr. Stuhlinger's proposed space ship would have the shape of a giant parasol.

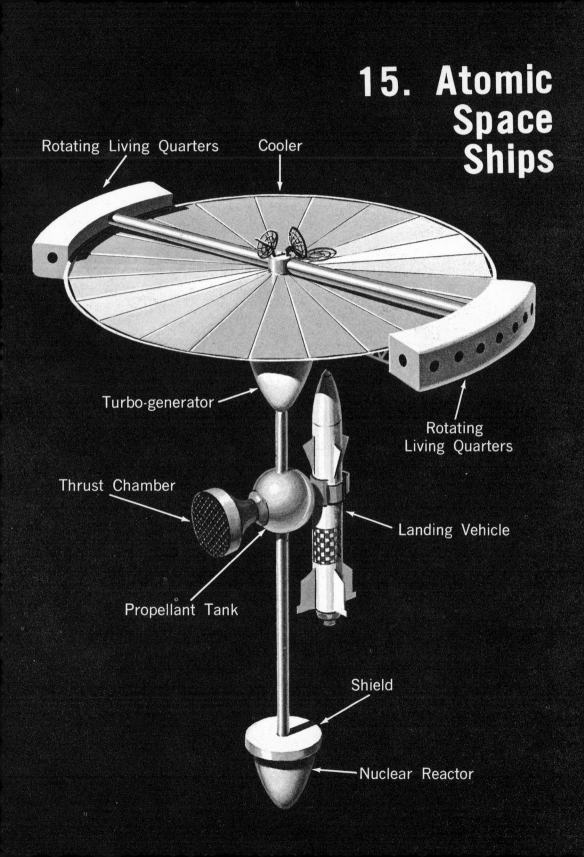

15. Atomic Space Ships

Rotating Living Quarters

Cooler

Turbo-generator

Thrust Chamber

Rotating Living Quarters

Landing Vehicle

Propellant Tank

Shield

Nuclear Reactor

Once the explorers of space have landed on the moon, their next goal will be the planet Mars.

However, it will be a much longer journey. The moon is only about 240,000 miles from the earth. Mars, at its closest approach to the earth, is 36,000,000 miles away.

Many scientists think that atomic energy will prove more satisfactory than liquid fuels as the source of power for a Martian space ship.

It may prove possible to launch a small Martian space ship directly from the surface of the earth with a big booster using atomic upper stages. Larger ships will have to be built at a space station and so will have to wait until such stations are in orbit around the earth.

The Martian space ship will use atomic energy in a quite different fashion from the atomic rockets discussed in Chapter 11. The atomic rocket constitutes a high-power system. It employs a nuclear reactor to heat a propellent gas to high temperature. The gas is then ejected from the nozzle of the rocket.

The atomic space ship, however, will be a low-power system. It will use a nuclear reactor to operate an electric power plant. Such a reactor can be quite small and can run at a fairly low temperature.

The heat of the reactor will be used to turn mercury into a vapor, which will operate a steam turbine. An electric generator, mounted on the shaft of the turbine, will produce an electric current. This current will make possible the operation of an ion engine, which will provide the motive power for the space ship. A model of one such engine has already been built at the Lewis Research Center of the NASA in Cleveland, Ohio.

The ion engine does not eject a train of heated gases as other rockets do. Instead it ejects a stream of electrified particles. The engine consists of two parts. There is a tank filled with some alkaline metal like cesium. This is heated just enough to cause the metal to vaporize. The vapor then enters a chamber where it comes in contact with a heated platinum grid.

This causes the cesium vapor to become ionized or electrified. The current produced by the electric generator is then used to speed up these electrified atoms or ions and to eject them from the nozzle of the engine.

The ion engine, because it has very little power, could not be used to lift a space ship off the ground against the earth's gravitational pull. But it is ideal for use in outer space. Whereas a chemical rocket burns up its fuel in a matter of minutes, an ion engine could be kept going during an entire flight. During the first half of a journey from the earth to Mars, it would accelerate or speed up the ship constantly. During the last half of the flight, it would slow up or decelerate the ship.

Another great advantage of the ion engine is the saving in weight.

A number of designs for atomic space ships have been

drawn by various scientists. One interesting design would look like a gigantic arrow. Perhaps the most interesting design is the one proposed by Dr. Ernst Stuhlinger of the Marshall Space Flight Center of the NASA in Huntsville, Alabama.

Imagine a gigantic umbrella 250 feet in diameter with a stick 250 feet long. That gives you an idea of this atomic space ship. It would weigh 730 tons.

The nuclear reactor in Dr. Stuhlinger's ship would be located at the bottom of the stick where you would find the handle of an ordinary umbrella.

Living quarters for the crew and passengers would be in cabins rotating around the top of the umbrella. This rotation would create a centrifugal force to relieve the sensation of weightlessness.

The heat of the reactor would be used to turn mercury into a vapor or steam. The steam would then go up a pipe through the stick of the umbrella and would operate a steam turbine just below the umbrella top.

An electric generator would be attached to the turbine. The energy of the nuclear reactor would be used, therefore, to generate electricity.

The top of the umbrella is really a great hollow vessel. The steam from the turbine would enter it. There it would cool very quickly, condensing into a liquid again. Then it would flow down a pipe in the stick of the umbrella, entering the nuclear reactor to be turned into steam once more.

The thrust chamber of the ion engine would be mounted on the stick halfway between the top of the umbrella and the handle. The electric current from the generator would operate it.

A space ship such as this would not be able to land on Mars. It would have to carry a small conventional rocket ship with wings to make the landing.

The big ship would go into an orbit around Mars and wait for the return of the explorers who made the landing. Then it would return to the terrestrial space station.

Our galaxy, the Milky Way, contains about a hundred billion stars, most of which are hundreds to thousands of light years away from us.

16. Exploring the Planets

Questions about our solar system that have long puzzled astronomers will be answered in the years ahead by unmanned space probes and by manned space ships.

This new way of exploring the solar system began when Russia launched Lunik I on January 2, 1959. It weighed 795 pounds and carried various scientific instruments.

It passed by the moon at a distance of about 3400 miles and then went into orbit around the sun, becoming the first artificial planet in history. Lunik I is now going around the sun in an orbit between that of the earth and Mars. It takes 443 days to go once around the sun.

Soon after, on March 3, 1959, the United States put a space probe, Pioneer IV, in a similar orbit. It passed by the moon at a distance of 37,000 miles and went into an orbit between those of the earth and of Mars. It takes 407 days to go once around the sun.

The United States put its second space probe into orbit around the sun on March 11, 1960. This became known as Pioneer V. Unlike Pioneer IV and Lunik I, whose orbits are between the earth and Mars, it is in orbit between the earth and Venus.

A three-stage Thor-Able rocket at Cape Canaveral was used to put Pioneer V into space. The launching was a triumph of rocket technique. After the third stage had burned out, separation of its shell from the satellite was effected by a radio command from the big radio telescope at Jodrell Bank in England.

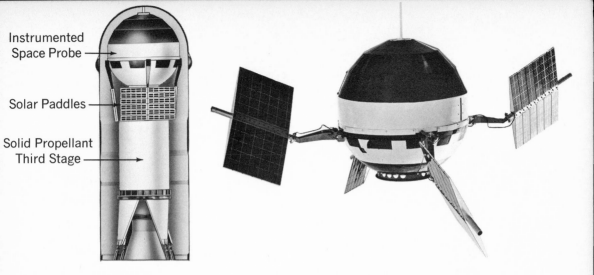

Instrumented
Space Probe

Solar Paddles

Solid Propellant
Third Stage

Diagram of Pioneer V (left above), showing its paddlewheels folded into the top stage of the Thor-Able launching rocket (below). The solar-cell paddlewheels (right above), which unfolded in space, powered the radio that sent signals to earth from 22 million miles away.

Pioneer V is a sphere 26 inches in diameter. Four paddlewheels with a wingspread of 4½ feet extend from it. These are covered with solar cells which charge the storage batteries that operate the radio.

There are two radios in Pioneer V. Because of battery failure, the larger radio did not work. But the smaller one, a five-watt transmitter, continued to send back data until Pioneer V was 22,500,000 miles from the earth. This was 50 times farther out in space than any previous satellite had been heard.

Russia put a space probe, Venus I, into orbit between

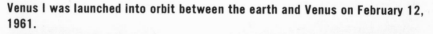

Venus I was launched into orbit between the earth and Venus on February 12, 1961.

the earth and Venus on February 12, 1961. The probe, which weighed approximately 1400 pounds, was a cylinder 80 inches long and 41 inches in diameter. Panels covered with solar cells and radio antennas were mounted on the exterior of the probe.

It was carried aloft in a satellite which was placed in orbit around the earth by a very large booster, probably a three-stage rocket. Then the probe was separated from the satellite and started on its way, probably by radio command from a Russian station.

The National Aeronautics and Space Administration has adopted a program for the exploration of the solar system which parallels its program for the study of the moon.

Probes like those planned for the lunar program will be used, with some modifications, in the planetary program. They will be launched with the same large boosters.

The first phase of this program has been named Project Mariner. It is planned to send space probes close enough to Venus and Mars to gather information about their temperatures, atmospheres, magnetic fields, and radiation belts.

The next phase will be known as Project Voyager. Its probes will eject capsules which will enter the atmospheres of Venus and Mars to collect more information about them.

Finally, after a manned space ship has gone around the moon, manned space ships will be sent to the neighborhoods of Venus and Mars.

Is there life on Mars? Perhaps this is the most exciting

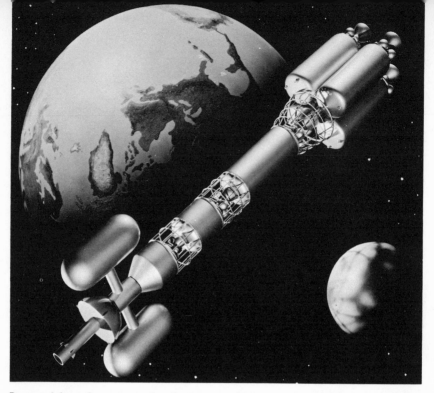

Proposal for a four-stage chemical space ship to carry an eight-man crew into orbit around Mars.

question awaiting an answer. Opinions have changed with each new discovery about the planet.

At the close of the last century, some astronomers were certain that Mars was inhabited by intelligent beings. Today most astronomers do not think so.

Mars has a diameter of 4,125 miles, a little more than half the diameter of the earth. A day on Mars is slightly longer than on earth, but a Martian year is almost equal to two of ours. Consequently each of the four seasons is almost twice as long on Mars as on earth.

Even a very small telescope reveals that Mars is an object of surprising beauty. The planet as a whole has a reddish or somewhat orange color when seen in the telescope.

However, an irregular belt running across the middle of the planet is darker in color, having bluish-gray, bluish-green, and greenish shades. The white polar caps are seen easily through a small telescope.

The reddish areas show very little change with the Martian seasons. Most astronomers are inclined to think that they are great rocky or sandy deserts.

With the approach of spring in the northern hemisphere of Mars, the polar cap begins to shrink and grow smaller. It may disappear entirely. At the same time, the green areas in the northern hemisphere grow darker in color and become more conspicuous. But in the autumn they begin to turn brown. At the same time, the polar cap grows larger.

The same changes take place in the southern hemisphere. However, just as on earth, it is winter in the southern hemisphere when it is summer in the northern hemisphere.

Watching these changes, it is easy to imagine that there is dense vegetation on Mars and that the planet must be inhabited.

In 1877 an Italian astronomer, G. V. Schiaparelli, announced that he had discovered a network of fine, straight lines on the surface of Mars. He called these *canali*, which is the Italian word for "channels." However, the word was translated as "canals."

This caused great excitement and made it more certain than ever in the minds of many people that the planet must be inhabited.

Astronomers are certain that Jupiter is very different from our earth. One theory is that it has a rocky core about 40,000 miles in diameter. This is covered by a layer of ice about 20,000 miles thick.

Above the ice there is an atmosphere of hydrogen gas in which float thick clouds of ammonia and methane. It is the outer surface of these clouds which we see in the telescope.

Astronomers believe that conditions on Saturn, Uranus, and Neptune are like those on Jupiter. All of these are too cold for life as we know it.

Little Pluto is the outermost planet of the solar system. It is so very far away that we know very little about it.

Perhaps you wonder what chance there is for space ships to leave the solar system and travel out among the stars. To answer this question we must know something about the distances of the stars.

The moon, you will recall, is about 240,000 miles away.

The sun is 93 million miles distant from us.

Pluto is more than 3½ billion miles away.

See how the scale of distances increases. First we used thousands of miles, then millions, then billions.

To measure the distances to the stars, we must use trillions of miles. The star nearest to our own sun is 25 trillion miles away.

Astronomers use a special yardstick, the light year—the

distance that light travels in a year. The speed of light is 186,000 miles a second. In a year, light travels six trillion miles.

Thus the next star is a little over four light years away. Other stars are ten light years away, still others 100 light years.

More than half the stars visible to the unaided eye are more than 400 light years away. The most distant stars in the Milky Way are about 100,000 light years away.

By now, you see the problem involved in journeying beyond the solar system. Even if we traveled with the amazing speed of light, it would still take us more than four years to reach the next star.

But nothing can travel as fast as light. This is one of the strange facts about the universe first pointed out by Dr. Albert Einstein in his theory of relativity. Someday it may be possible to build space ships that will travel almost as fast as light.

We must remember that the Age of Space Travel is very, very young. The first artificial satellites were launched in 1957. The years ahead will see amazing progress and equally amazing discoveries about the wonderful universe in which we live.

Appendix

Some Important Spacecraft

	Date Launched	Launching Rocket
Research Satellites		
Sputnik I (USSR)	Oct. 4, 1957	*Not disclosed*
Sputnik II (USSR)	Nov. 3, 1957	*Not disclosed*
Explorer I (U.S.)	Jan. 31, 1958	Jupiter C
Vanguard I (U.S.)	Mar. 17, 1958	Vanguard
Explorer III (U.S.)	Mar. 26, 1958	Jupiter C
Sputnik III (USSR)	May 15, 1958	*Not disclosed*
Explorer IV (U.S.)	July 26, 1958	Jupiter C
Vanguard III (U.S.)	Sept. 18, 1959	Vanguard
Explorer VII (U.S.)	Oct. 13, 1959	Juno II
Explorer VIII (U.S.)	Nov. 3, 1960	Juno II
Explorer X (U.S.)	Mar. 25, 1961	Thor-Delta
Explorer XI (U.S.)	Apr. 27, 1961	Juno II
Explorer XII (U.S.)	Aug. 15, 1961	Thor-Delta
Explorer XIII (U.S.)	Aug. 25, 1961	Scout
Earth Observation Satellites		
Explorer VI (U.S.)	Aug. 7, 1959	Thor-Able III
Tiros I (U.S.)	Apr. 1, 1960	Thor-Able
Tiros II (U.S.)	Nov. 23, 1960	Thor-Delta
Tiros III (U.S.)	July 12, 1961	Thor-Delta
Communications Satellites		
Transit I-B (U.S.)	Apr. 13, 1960	Thor-Able-Star
Transit II-A (U.S.)	June 22, 1960	Thor-Able-Star

Payload Weight in Pounds	Result
184	*Measured density of upper atmosphere*
1,120	*Carried dog; observed cosmic rays*
30.8	*Discovered inner Van Allen belt*
3.25	*Revealed earth is pear-shaped*
31	*Observed inner Van Allen belt, micrometeorites*
2,925	*Observed cosmic rays, micrometeorites*
38.4	*Observed inner Van Allen belt*
100	*Observed earth's magnetic field, solar X-rays*
91.5	*Observed solar radiation outbursts*
90.14	*Observed ionosphere*
78	*Observed Van Allen belts, magnetic fields*
82	*Observed high-energy gamma rays*
83	*Observed solar radiation, magnetic fields, Van Allen belts*
187	*Observed micrometeorites*
142	*First crude television pictures of earth*
270	*Weather eye; photographed cloud cover*
280	*Weather eye; photographed cloud cover, mapped infrared radiation from earth*
285	*Photographed cloud cover, measured solar energy absorbed, reflected, and emitted by earth*
265	*Global navigational satellite*
223 & 42	*Two satellites: larger, navigational; smaller, observed solar radiation*

	Date Launched	*Launching Rocket*
Echo I (U.S.)	Aug. 12, 1960	Thor-Delta
Courier I-B (U.S.)	Oct. 4, 1960	Thor-Able-Star

Space Probes

	Date Launched	*Launching Rocket*
Pioneer III (U.S.)	Dec. 6, 1958	Juno II
Lunik I (USSR)	Jan. 2, 1959	*Not disclosed*
Pioneer IV (U.S.)	Mar. 3, 1959	Juno II
Lunik II (USSR)	Sept. 12, 1959	*Not disclosed*
Lunik III (USSR)	Oct. 4, 1959	*Not disclosed*
Pioneer V (U.S.)	Mar. 11, 1960	Thor-Able IV
Venus I (USSR)	Feb. 12, 1961	*Not disclosed*

Recovery Projects

	Date Launched	*Launching Rocket*
Discoverer XIII (U.S.)	Aug. 10, 1960	Thor-Agena
Discoverer XIV (U.S.)	Aug. 18, 1960	Thor-Agena
Spacecraft II (USSR)	Aug. 19, 1960	*Not disclosed*
Discoverer XVII (U.S.)	Nov. 12, 1960	Thor-Agena
Discoverer XVIII (U.S.)	Dec. 7, 1960	Thor-Agena
Mercury (U.S.)	Jan. 31, 1961	Redstone
Spacecraft IV (USSR)	Mar. 9, 1961	*Not disclosed*
Spacecraft V (USSR)	Mar. 25, 1961	*Not disclosed*
Discoverer XXXV (U.S.)	Nov. 15, 1961	Thor-Agena
Mercury-Atlas V (U.S.)	Nov. 29, 1961	Atlas D

Man Into Space

	Date Launched	*Launching Rocket*
Vostok I (USSR)	Apr. 12, 1961	*Not disclosed*
Freedom-7 (U.S.)	May 5, 1961	Redstone
Liberty Bell-7 (U.S.)	July 21, 1961	Redstone
Vostok II (USSR)	Aug. 6, 1961	*Not disclosed*
Friendship-7 (U.S.)	Feb. 20, 1962	Atlas

Payload Weight in Pounds	Result
132	Passive communications satellite for radio and TV
500	Active communications satellite; relayed radio messages
12.95	Discovered outer Van Allen belt
795	Went into solar orbit
13.4	Went into solar orbit
858.4	Hit moon on Sept. 13, 1959
614	Photographed hidden side of moon
94.8	Went into solar orbit; transmitted data from 22,500,000 miles
1,419	Went into solar orbit
1,700	Capsule recovered from ocean
1,700	Capsule retrieved in mid-air by airplane
10,120	Cabin containing two dogs recovered
2,100	Capsule retrieved in mid-air
2,100	Capsule retrieved in mid-air
2,000	Chimpanzee given ride over Atlantic Missile Range
10,340	Cabin containing dog recovered
10,330	Cabin containing dog recovered
2,100	Capsule retrieved
2,900	Chimpanzee orbited earth twice and returned
10,418	Major Yuri Gagarin orbited earth once and returned
2,900	Commander Alan B. Shepard, Jr., made flight over Atlantic Missile Range
2,900	Captain Virgil I. Grissom made flight over Atlantic Missile Range
10,430	Major Gherman Titov orbited earth 17½ times and returned
2,900	Lieut. Colonel John H. Glenn, Jr., orbited earth three times and returned

Index

The Author

David Dietz, winner of the Pulitzer Prize in Journalism, has also received the Westinghouse Distinguished Science Writers Award, the American Chemical Society's Grady Award, and the Lasker Medical Journalism Award. He is a member of the editorial staff of the Cleveland *Press*, as well as science editor of the Scripps-Howard newspapers.

Dr. Dietz is a fellow of the American Association for the Advancement of Science, the Ohio Academy of Science, and the Royal Astronomical Society of Great Britain. He is also a member of the American Astronomical Society and the Société Astronomique de France. He is the author of several books, including *All About Great Medical Discoveries*.